What's there to do on a boring evening? You can watch mindless TV shows—or treat yourself to some refreshing mental exercise! When you're sitting in a dreary waiting room, do you get tired of reading old worn-out magazines? Then take along these enjoyable brainteasers and relax before your appointment! Would you like to brighten the afternoons of sick or shut-in loved ones? Give them these challenging puzzles that will keep them occupied with Bible-centered fun! There's no end to the uses and occasions for this collection of all-new puzzles. Be sure to keep this book handy at all times!

The Bible Puzzle Book

Marcina Gay

SPIRE BOOKS

Fleming H. Revell Company
Old Tappan, New Jersey

Scripture quotations are based on the King James Version of the Bible.

ISBN 0-8007-8487-1

A Spire Book
Copyright © 1984 by Marcina Gay
All rights reserved
Printed in the United States of America

This is an original Spire book, published by Spire Books, a division of Fleming H. Revell Company, Old Tappan, New Jersey

Contents

The Bible
Puzzle Book

They Were Writers

We have our Bible today because many men took the time to write. How much do you know about those men? Some names may appear more than once.

1. This writer was known as the first missionary.
2. This writer is commonly known as the "weeping prophet."
3. You may notice several medical terms and stories when you read this man's work.
4. This writer lost everything he had because he loved and served the living God.
5. This man led his people out of bondage.
6. After the death of Moses, this man led the children of Israel into the Promised Land.
7. This Old Testament writer was a scribe.
8. This writer has been considered the wisest man who ever lived.
9. A New Testament writer, he was Jesus' half-brother.
10. In his weakness, this writer denied ever knowing Jesus.
11. A prophet, this writer was deserted by his wife.
12. First a shepherd and later a king, this writer wrote most of the Psalms.
13. This writer was a military leader under Moses.
14. This writer was a brother of Jesus.
15. The writer of the last book of the Bible.
16. This writer was a prophet and a herdsman.
17. This writer was released from prison by an angel.
18. This man claimed to be a bondslave of Christ.
19. This writer's book was one of Jesus' favorite books.
20. He was banished to the Isle of Patmos for preaching.

Teachings of the Beatitudes

The nine beatitudes describe those who are truly happy. Can you match the phrases below to complete the beatitudes?

1. Blessed are the poor in spirit. . . .
2. Blessed are those who mourn. . . .
3. Blessed are the meek. . . .
4. Blessed are those who hunger and thirst after righteousness. . . .
5. Blessed are the merciful. . . .
6. Blessed are the pure in heart. . . .
7. Blessed are the peacemakers. . . .
8. Blessed are those who are persecuted for righteousness' sake. . . .
9. Blessed are you when men revile and persecute you and utter all kinds of evil about you for my name's sake. . . .

a. for they shall inherit the earth.
b. for they shall be called the children of God.
c. for theirs is the kingdom of heaven.
d. for they shall obtain mercy.
e. for your reward is in heaven.
f. for they shall be comforted.
g. for they shall see God.
h. for they shall be satisfied.

Where Is It?

How quickly could you answer if someone were to ask you where the following stories could be found in the Bible? These are a little tough, but see how many you can answer correctly.

1. Life of Samuel
2. Paul's shipwreck
3. A queen's love for her people
4. The story of the flood
5. A runaway slave
6. Anointing of David as king
7. The Garden of Gethsemane
8. Sermon on the Mount
9. The conversion of Paul
10. The Good Samaritan
11. Giving of the Ten Commandments
12. The love chapter
13. The call of Abraham
14. Christ's Ascension
15. Palm Sunday
16. Jonah and the whale
17. Children in the fiery furnace
18. Death of Saul
19. Samson's courtship and marriage
20. David and Goliath
21. Battle of Armageddon
22. The Last Supper
23. The raising of Lazarus from the dead
24. Sighting of the first rainbow
25. Parting of the Red Sea

The Psalms of David

David uses many phrases to show the relationship between God and His children. See how many Scripture phrases you can complete.

1. The Lord is my _____; I shall not want.
2. O Lord our _____, how excellent is thy name in all the earth.
3. Let the words of my mouth, and the meditation of my heart, be acceptable in thy sight, O Lord, my strength, and my _____.
4. O God, thou art my _____; early will I seek thee. . . .
5. Lift up your heads, O ye gates; even lift them up, ye everlasting doors; and the _____ of glory shall come in.
6. God is our _____ and strength, a very present help in trouble.
7. But thou, O Lord, art a _____ for me; my glory, and the lifter up of my head.
8. The Lord is my light and my _____. . . .
9. I will say unto God, my _____, Why hast thou forgotten me? . . .
10. Be thou my strong rock, for an _____ of defence to save me.
11. Lord, thou hast been our _____ _____. . . .
12. The Lord is thy _____; the Lord is thy shade upon thy right hand.
13. The Lord is my strength and _____. . . .
14. The Lord is my _____, and my _____, and my _____.
15. The Lord is their _____, and he is the saving strength of his anointed.
16. He is my _____, and there is no unrighteousness in him.
17. For the Lord God is a _____ and shield. . . .
18. For God is my _____ of old, working salvation in the midst of the earth.
19. But God is the _____. . . .
20. A _____ of the fatherless, and a _____ of the widows, is God in his holy habitation.

Professional Skills

If people in the Bible were living today, who might you ask to do the following skills? There may be several correct answers, but the most popular name has been given here.

1. Build a tent for you to take camping.
2. Set a broken bone.
3. Go out from your church and preach in a foreign country.
4. Figure out how much tax you owe.
5. Accompany you on a deep-sea-fishing vacation.
6. Tutor you in the Hebrew Law.
7. Bargain for you at a big sale.
8. Give advice on handling your house staff.
9. Guide you on a tour of the country.
10. Give instructions on making a waterproof cradle.
11. Teach you the skills of the hunter.
12. Watch over your animals when you are away.
13. Explain the meaning of a strange dream.
14. Alter a new dress you just bought.
15. Show you the best way to plant your vegetables.
16. Build you new kitchen cabinets.
17. Hold a revival in your church.
18. Make you a beautiful silver tea set.
19. Take over the administration of your affairs during a lengthy leave of absence.
20. Send out as a spy from your company.

It Was Romance

How many of these lovers are you able to pair up? Some wives may not be the most popular one that a particular man had.

1. Rebekah
2. Jacob
3. Zacharias
4. Joseph
5. Ananias
6. Samson
7. Elkanah
8. Abraham
9. Ruth
10. David
11. Ahab
12. Naomi
13. Zebedee
14. Eve
15. Herod Antipas
16. Solomon
17. Maacah
18. Lamech
19. Priscilla
20. Jehoram

a. Mary
b. Adam
c. Isaac
d. Jezebel
e. Michal
f. Delilah
g. Herodias
h. Elimelech
i. Salome
j. Zillah
k. Rachel
l. Naamah

m. Rehoboam
n. Sapphira
o. Athaliah
p. Boaz
q. Aquila
r. Hannah
s. Sarah
t. Elizabeth

Categorize That Book

The books of the Old Testament have been divided into five categories. See how many books you can identify correctly.

1. Joshua
2. Psalms
3. Job
4. Genesis
5. Isaiah
6. Ezekiel
7. Amos
8. Ruth
9. Lamentations
10. Proverbs
11. Nahum
12. Numbers
13. Ecclesiastes
14. Daniel
15. Esther
16. Jonah
17. 1 Kings
18. Song of Solomon
19. Joel
20. Exodus
21. Jeremiah
22. Haggai
23. Leviticus
24. Ezra
25. Malachi

a. Law
b. History
c. Poetry and Wisdom
d. Major prophets
e. Minor prophets

Kings and Queens

Royalty is enchanting to many people, and we tend to stand back and view it with awe. Try to identify the royal members below.

1. This king owned 900 chariots of iron.
2. He put Daniel into the den of lions for a night.
3. This man became the first king of Israel.
4. She became queen in a foreign country.
5. This king was killed in his drunkenness.
6. A queen who was eaten by dogs.
7. She was the queen of Ethiopia.
8. The wife of King Agrippa.
9. A king who rode on a ferryboat across the Jordan River.
10. Daniel interpreted the handwriting on the wall for this king.
11. She told her daughter to ask for the head of John the Baptist.
12. She killed her whole family so she could become queen.
13. He became king at seven years of age.
14. He became king at eight years of age.
15. This queen was Solomon's mother.
16. She was removed from being queen because she made an idol.
17. This king brought water into the city.
18. He exceeded all the kings of the earth in riches.
19. She tested King Solomon with difficult questions.
20. He provoked God to anger more than any other king.

Who Am I?

This quiz involves anyone and everyone. In fact, it's fairly easy. Try to get a perfect score.

1. My wife became a pillar of salt.
2. I was beheaded in prison.
3. Paul and I sang while in prison.
4. I was the first son of Adam and Eve.
5. I committed suicide by falling on my own sword.
6. I sold Jesus for thirty pieces of silver.
7. I walked naked for three years.
8. I anointed Jesus' feet with costly perfume.
9. I washed the disciples' feet, showing a spirit of humility.
10. I grieved when my sons showed me a blood-soaked coat.
11. Earlier one of Jesus' disciples, I was banished to the Isle of Patmos.
12. I was David's best friend.
13. I traveled to a foreign land to meet my husband.
14. I was a twin to Jacob.
15. God changed my name to Paul.
16. I am called "the father of many nations."
17. Jesus asked me to take care of His mother.
18. I announced the birth of Jesus to Mary.
19. I revived a dead man in church.
20. I saw a bush on fire, although it never burned up.
21. I didn't like it that my sister wouldn't help me with the housework.
22. I denied Jesus three times in one night.
23. I was the father of King David.
24. I was stricken with leprosy because I spoke against Moses.
25. Jesus raised me from the dead.
26. I was hanged on the gallows I had built for someone else.
27. I was given to David as a wife in reward for his slaying Goliath.

28. God found me to be a righteous man in a very corrupt age.
29. I gave my maid to my husband for a wife, since I could have no children.
30. I gave my son to become the Redeemer of mankind.

Some Tricky Items

The answers to these clues are pretty difficult; if you can answer them, you can feel pretty smart.

1. The name given to a female slave.
2. Abraham used one for a dwelling place.
3. Jonah was overcome by it.
4. Sunday is the day for this.
5. A writer and transcriber of the law.
6. A Roman coin.
7. A stringed musical instrument.
8. An animal often used for a sacrifice.
9. A sacred vestment worn by the high priest.
10. Court of the high priest's palace.
11. Lodging place for travelers.
12. The characteristic teaching method of Jesus.
13. Referred to as having two edges.
14. Ordinary form of capital punishment.
15. Building to feed and keep animals in.
16. Another name for bulrushes.
17. Used as a place of refuge.
18. A word meaning "love."
19. A venomous serpent.
20. Was used to tell time during the day.
21. A rod carried in the hand.
22. A shallow place in a stream, where men and animals could cross on foot.
23. A large piece of timber, used in a figurative sense by Jesus.
24. A medicinal balsam.

Dreams and Dreamers

Can you match the dreamers with their dreams? Some names may be used more than once.

1. His wife received a divine message in a dream.
2. This man was called "the dreamer."
3. He dreamed of angels ascending and descending on a ladder.
4. He said a dream may come through a multitude of business.
5. The only interpreter of dreams.
6. God told him in a dream that the woman he had taken was another man's wife.
7. He dreamed of seven good ears of corn and seven bad ears of corn.
8. They were told to go home a different way than planned.
9. In a dream he asked for understanding of his people.
10. He saw ringstraked cattle.
11. The sun, moon, and stars bowed down to him in a dream.
12. He saw four great beasts in a dream.
13. He was instructed to send men to Joppa to find a man named Peter.
14. He had a vision of unclean beasts and, though instructed to eat, would not.
15. He saw in a vision a man crying for him to come over into Macedonia.

a. Joseph
b. God
c. Jacob
d. Wise men
e. Pilate
f. Solomon
g. Daniel
h. Abimelech

i. Pharaoh
j. Peter
k. Cornelius
l. Paul

What's That in Your Hand?

When you think of a rod, you think of Moses. Can you match the names and symbols below?

1. Ark
2. Harp
3. Purple cloth
4. Rod
5. Two spies
6. Sackcloth
7. Locusts and wild honey
8. Coat of many colors
9. Frankincense
10. Wisdom
11. Lion's den
12. Ravens
13. Golden calf
14. Carpenter shop
15. Chariots
16. Whale
17. Facial makeup
18. Lame feet
19. Bow and arrow
20. Foxes

a. Moses
b. Rahab
c. Solomon
d. Magi
e. Aaron
f. Jehu
g. Joseph
h. Mephibosheth
i. Job
j. Jonathan
k. Noah
l. Daniel
m. Jesus

n. Lydia
o. Jezebel
p. John the Baptist
q. David
r. Samson
s. Jonah
t. Elijah

Remember the Trees?

Surprisingly, a lot of situations in the Bible centered around a tree. Can you identify the trees? Try them.

1. A carpenter planted this tree.
2. This kind of tree was planted by an eagle.
3. An angel stood among these trees.
4. A king tarried under this tree.
5. Absalom got his hair caught in this tree.
6. The Bible speaks of beating this tree.
7. Zacchaeus climbed up into this tree so he could see Jesus.
8. Twigs from this tree were planted and grew into a vine.
9. This tree conferred immortality on persons eating its fruits.
10. Solomon used this tree to make doors in the temple.
11. People waved branches from this tree as Jesus rode into Jerusalem.
12. This tree was called the king of trees in the fable in the book of Judges.
13. This tree served as an instrument to test the obedience of Adam and Eve.
14. Noah used this tree to build the ark.
15. Elijah sat underneath this kind of tree.
16. A hill looking over the city of Jerusalem is the name of this tree.
17. Jesus cursed this tree, and it died.
18. Solomon used its wood to build the temple.
19. This tree had a part in David's beating the Philistines.
20. The exiled Jews hung their harps on the branches of this tree.

They Were First

Sometimes, first things are easier to remember, like the first book of the Bible or the first president of the United States. Many events in the Bible are known for being the first. Can you identify them?

1. First man
2. First woman
3. First murderer
4. First rainfall
5. First city
6. First of the ten plagues
7. Wore the first bridal veil
8. First exile
9. First hunter
10. First shepherd
11. First historian
12. Told the first lie
13. First high priest
14. First scriptural song
15. First mountain mentioned
16. Wore the first ring
17. First shepherdess
18. First king of Israel
19. First judge of Israel
20. First disciple chosen
21. First missionary
22. First missionary meeting
23. Town of Jesus' first miracle
24. First church
25. First Christian martyr
26. First book of the Old Testament
27. First book of the New Testament
28. First book of prophecy
29. First book named after a woman
30. First church picnic

They Have Feathers

Birds played a part, too. Match them up.

1. Peter denied Jesus thrice before it crowed.
2. This bird brought food to Elijah.
3. God sent it to the Israelites for food.
4. It brought an olive leaf to the ark.
5. This bird is thought to be very proud.
6. A blind bird.
7. This bird is very wise.
8. Jesus mentioned it as He looked over Jerusalem.
9. This bird is a type of vulture.
10. A bird with strong, mighty wings.
11. You could buy two for a farthing.
12. This bird was forbidden as food.
13. An aquatic bird.
14. A carnivorous bird.
15. A large aquatic bird.
16. This bird was used as a sacrifice.
17. A migratory bird.
18. A large bird of prey.

a. Quail
b. Bat
c. Chicken
d. Falcon
e. Cock
f. Cuckoo
g. Peacock
h. Pigeon
i. Sparrow
j. Raven
k. Heron
l. Owl
m. Vulture
n. Dove
o. Eagle
p. Pelican
q. Stork
r. Crane

Hunter's Choice

There are many animals named in the Bible. Just a few of them are mentioned below. See how many of them you can guess.

1. Joseph's brothers dipped his coat in the blood of this animal.
2. In Proverbs, a busybody is likened to one who takes this animal by the ears.
3. Joseph was given these by the Egyptians.
4. Jesus caused evil spirits to enter a herd of them.
5. This animal was once miraculously killed by David.
6. Jesus refers to His children as this kind of animal.
7. A beast of burden.
8. John the Baptist wore garments made of the hair of this animal.
9. One fastened itself to Paul's hand.
10. Samson used these animals to burn the field of the Philistines.
11. Jeremiah stated that this animal is swifter than an eagle.
12. This animal is known as the king of beasts.
13. Aaron made a golden image of this animal.

Complete the Verse

Many Scripture verses are very familiar to us, and many have been committed to memory. Read each verse below and fill in the missing word or words.

1. O death, where is thy _____? O grave, where is thy _____?

   1 Corinthians 15:55

2. For they that wait upon the Lord shall renew their _____; they shall mount up with _____ as eagles; they shall run, and not be _____; and they shall walk and not _____.

   Isaiah 40:31

3. Then spake Jesus again unto them, saying, "I am the _____ of the world: he that followeth me shall not walk in _____ but shall have the light of _____.

   John 8:12

4. Let not your _____ be troubled: ye believe in God, believe also in me.

   John 14:1

5. In the beginning, God _____ the heaven and the earth.

   Genesis 1:1

6. Jesus _____.

   John 11:35

7. In my Father's _____ are many _____: if it were not so, I would have told you. I go to _____ a place for you.

   John 14:2

8. Make a joyful _____ unto the Lord, all ye lands.

   Psalms 100:1

9. Thy _____ is a _____ unto my feet, and a _____ unto my _____.

   Psalms 119:105

10. If we _____ our sins, he is _____ and just to forgive us our sins, and to _____ us from all unrighteousness.

    1 John 1:9

11. For to me to _____ is Christ, and to _____ is
_____.

12. And they said, _____ on the Lord Jesus Christ, and
thou shalt be saved, and thy _____.

Acts 16:31

13. Beloved, if God so _____ us, we ought also to _____
one another.

1 John 4:11

14. He who sitteth in the heavens shall _____: the Lord
shall have them in _____.

Psalms 2:4

15. He giveth _____ to the faint; and to those who have no
might he increaseth _____.

Isaiah 40:29

16. For this is my _____ of the new testament, which is
shed for the remission of _____.

Matthew 26:28

17. If ye love me, keep my _____.

John 14:15

18. I can do _____ things through Christ which _____
me.

Philippians 4:13

19. For the which cause I also suffer these things: neverthe-
less, I am not _____: for I know whom I have _____,
and am persuaded that he is able to keep that which I
have _____ unto him against that day.

2 Timothy 1:12

20. For whosoever shall keep the whole law, and yet offend in _____ point, he is _____ of all.

James 2:10

21. I will say of the Lord, He is my _____ and my _____:
my God; in him will I _____.

Psalms 91:2

22. I have fought a good _____, I have finished my
_____, I have kept the _____.

2 Timothy 4:7

23. Great is the _____, and greatly to be _____ in the city
of our God, in the _____ of his holiness.

Psalms 48:1

30

24. God is our _____ and _____, a very present _____ in trouble.

Psalms 46:1

25. The ungodly are not so: but are like the _____ which the _____ driveth away.

Psalms 1:4

Who Said It?

What persons in the Bible made the following statements?

1. Entreat me not to leave thee . . . thy people shall be my people, and thy God my God.
2. Father, forgive them; for they know not what they do.
3. The Lord is my shepherd.
4. Pride goeth before destruction, and an haughty spirit before a fall.
5. I press toward the mark for the prize of the high calling of God in Christ Jesus.
6. O Jerusalem, Jerusalem, . . . how often would I have gathered thy children together, even as a hen gathereth her chickens under her wings.
7. Lord, lay not this sin to their charge.
8. Am I my brother's keeper?
9. Saul, Saul, why persecutest thou me?
10. What I have written I have written.
11. Truly, this man was the Son of God.
12. There cometh one mightier than I after me.
13. Thou art my beloved Son, in whom I am well pleased.
14. Lord, by this time he stinketh: for he hath been dead four days.
15. Lord, we know not where thou goest; and how can we know the way?
16. Lord, I will lay down my life for thy sake.
17. Who shall separate us from the love of Christ?
18. Prepare ye the way of the Lord.
19. How can a man be born when he is old?
20. Woman, what have I to do with thee?
21. We are troubled on every side, yet not distressed; we are perplexed, but not in despair.
22. Out of the depths have I cried unto thee, O Lord.
23. How long will ye vex my soul, and break me in pieces with words?
24. Let my life be given me at my petition, and my people at my request.
25. Watch and pray, that ye enter not into temptation; the spirit indeed is willing, but the flesh is weak.

Name the Song

Many songs have been sung so often that we can name the title from listening to the first line. The first lines to some old songs have been given. Read each and see if you can guess the song's title.

1. Jesus, keep me near the cross, There a precious fountain.
2. All to Jesus I surrender; All to Him I freely give.
3. When He cometh, when He cometh, To make up His jewels.
4. Praise God, from whom all blessings flow; Praise Him all creatures here below.
5. Brightly beams our Father's mercy, From His lighthouse evermore.
6. I've found a Friend in Jesus. He's everything to me.
7. Sowing in the morning, sowing seeds of kindness.
8. There comes to my heart one sweet strain, A glad and a joyous refrain.
9. When morning gilds the skies: My heart awaking cries.
10. Encamped along the hills of light, Ye Christian soldiers rise.
11. What can wash away my sin?
12. I stand amazed in the presence of Jesus the Nazarene.
13. We have heard the joyful sound.
14. The whole world was lost in the darkness of sin.
15. I know not why God's wondrous grace, To me He hath made known.
16. Far away in the depths of my spirit tonight, Rolls a melody sweeter than psalm.
17. I have found His grace in all complete; He supplieth ev'ry need.
18. Low in the grave He lay—Jesus my Saviour.
19. I cannot tell the whence it came, This peace within my breast.
20. Sing the wondrous love of Jesus; Sing His mercy and His grace.
21. Mine eyes have seen the glory of the coming of the Lord.

22. When we walk with the Lord In the light of His Word, What a glory He sheds on our way!

23. I'm pressing on the upward way, New heights I'm gaining every day.

24. God's abiding peace is in my soul today. Yes, I feel it now.

25. A wonderful Saviour is Jesus, my Lord, A wonderful Saviour to me.

26. My heart was distressed 'neath Jehovah's dread frown; And low in the pit where my sins dragged me down.

27. It may not be on the mountain height, Or over the stormy sea.

28. Would you be free from your burden of sin?

29. There's a land that is fairer than day, And by faith we can see it afar.

30. I'm rejoicing night and day, As I walk the pilgrim way.

31. What a fellowship, what a joy divine.

32. Oh, spread the tidings 'round, wherever man is found.

33. My hope is built on nothing less Than Jesus' blood and righteousness.

34. Alas! and did my Saviour bleed, And did my sovereign die?

35. Years I spent in vanity and pride, Caring not my Lord was crucified.

36. My soul in sad exile was out on life's sea, So burdened with sin and distrest.

37. When peace like a river attendeth my way, When sorrows like sea billows roll.

38. In shady green pastures so rich and so sweet.

39. My Father is rich in houses and lands; He holdeth the wealth of the world in His hands!

40. When the trumpet of the Lord shall sound, and time shall be no more.

41. Upon life's boundless ocean where mighty billows roll.

42. We praise Thee, O God, For the Son of Thy love, For Jesus, who died and is now gone above.

43. All my life long I had panted for a draught from some cool spring.

44. The Lord is my Shepherd; I shall not want.

45. For God so loved this sinful world, His Son He freely gave.

A Look at Mothers

Mothers are special, and we commemorate them with a special day. How many Bible mothers can you identify by the clues given below? Some names may appear more than once.

1. This mother was accused of being drunk while praying for a son. *Hannah*
2. This concubine had a son named *Ishmael*. *Hagar*
3. Fearful that her baby would be killed, she hid him among the tall grasses in the river. *Jochebed*
4. This mother's son was the forerunner of Jesus. *Elizabeth*
5. After traveling for many miles, this mother gave birth in a lowly stable. *Mary*
6. This mother's son became the first murderer. *Eve*
7. Because she was so old, this mother laughed when she found out she was going to have a child. *Sarah*
8. When her husband was dying, this mother encouraged her son to trick his father and gain the birthright.
9. This mother was the great-grandmother of King David.
10. This mother's son was known for his wisdom.
11. She was the very first mother. *Eve*
12. This Jewish mother gave her son to help Paul in his missionary work. He became like a son to the missionary.
13. This mother instructed her daughter to ask for the head of John the Baptist. *Herodias*
14. This mother was honored above all women. *Mary*
15. She was the mother of twin boys. *Rebekah*

35

What Did They Eat?

Not many foods in Bible times were the same as ours today. Do you know what they are? How many of them would you like to try?

1. This man refused to eat the king's rich food.
2. They were a bit of protein for John the Baptist.
3. God gave it to the children of Israel each morning.
4. The very poor people in the Old Testament could offer a handful of it for a sacrifice.
5. Jesus shared it with Judas at the passover meal.
6. A young lad had two of them.
7. This was given to Jesus to drink when He was on the cross.
8. Elijah was sustained in a widow's home; God increased her meal and _____ each day.
9. This food is called "the staff of life."
10. A word used to refer to all kinds of grain.
11. Jesse sent David to his brothers with ten of them.
12. Solomon wrote that he had drunk it with his wine.
13. Job said he had been curdled like it.
14. Daniel and his four companions became "fairer in countenance" living on this type of diet.
15. Job suggests that eggs should be eaten with it.
16. Samson took some to his parents.
17. Jonathan nearly lost his life by breaking the king's command and eating it.
18. Jesus said we are the _____ of the earth.
19. "Give us this day our daily _____."
20. Jesus prepared these for His apostles one morning for breakfast as they came onto shore from a night of fishing.
21. Jesus cursed this tree.
22. This satisfied John the Baptist's sweet tooth.
23. Hosea said the tribe of Ephraim was a half-baked one.
24. The Kingdom of Heaven is said to be like a grain of this seed.
25. Perhaps you think of one of Noah's sons when you eat this kind of meat.

April Fools' Day

We think of April Fools' Day as a time for pulling tricks on others. The following people tricked someone or were tricked by someone. Do you know who?

1. The witch of En-dor was tricked by him.
2. He was tricked into marrying the wrong daughter.
3. He was tricked by his son.
4. He was tricked by false prophets.
5. He was tricked by a woman.
6. She tricked the townspeople who were looking for the spies.
7. He and his wife sold their land for a different price from the one they quoted.
8. He tried to trick Jesus in the wilderness.
9. She was tricked into eating forbidden fruit.
10. His father was tricked into thinking he was dead.
11. She tricked her husband into stealing Naboth's vineyard.
12. A young girl who tricked the king's daughter.
13. They tried to trick Jesus with Roman coins.
14. He was tricked by a silver cup in his sack of grain.
15. He was tricked by his daughter who had stolen his god.
16. He was tricked by a woman who ran a spike through his head.
17. He tricked the king into believing that his wife was his sister.
18. He tried to trick the wise men into believing he wanted to worship the baby Jesus, too.
19. He outsmarted his enemies by escaping over the wall in a basket.
20. She deceived the soldiers of Saul by placing a false image of her husband in his bed.

a. Isaac
b. Eve
c. Rahab
d. Jezebel
e. Sisera

f. King Saul
g. Benjamin
h. Ananias
i. Miriam
j. Laban
k. Samson
l. Pharisees
m. Abraham
n. Jacob
o. Joseph
p. Michal
q. Herod
r. Satan
s. Paul
t. Balaam

A Look at Fathers

Fathers are to be the head of the home. How many biblical fathers can you identify?

1. To show his love for God, this man was willing to offer his son as a sacrifice.
2. This young father had a son who was lame in both feet.
3. This father tried to kill his son's best friend.
4. Father of the first murderer.
5. A priest who was the father of John the Baptist.
6. He gave his favorite son a beautiful coat.
7. This father tricked the man who became his son-in-law.
8. Jesus brought this man's daughter back to life.
9. The Father of all mankind.
10. This father taught his son the skills of a carpenter.
11. A father who saved his sons from a great flood.
12. This man's son killed a giant.
13. This father had twin sons.
14. This father led the Israelite children out of Egypt.
15. This father's son made the sun stand still.
16. The father of a very strong man.
17. The father of James and John.
18. This father was once a musician in Saul's court.
19. This father was a priest in the temple where Hannah prayed.
20. This father was forbidden to mourn the death of his son.

New Testament Persons

New Testament persons may be a bit more familiar to some than those in the Old Testament. Take this quiz and then the next one and find out which book is most familiar to you.

1. She invited Paul to stay in her home in Thyatira.
2. He was the father of James and John.
3. This man came to see Jesus during the night.
4. This man was "almost persuaded" after hearing Paul's case.
5. He was raised from the dead after three days.
6. He sought to kill the baby Jesus.
7. This girl recognized Peter upon his release from prison.
8. Although a member of the Sanhedrin, this man believed Jesus to be the Messiah.
9. This disciple wasn't sure Jesus had really risen.
10. A beggar who lay at Abraham's bosom.
11. He witnessed Jesus' transfiguration with Peter and John.
12. The first to see the risen Lord.
13. Jesus was condemned for eating at his home with publicans and sinners.
14. The disciples let him down in a basket at night so he could escape from the city.
15. A sister to Martha and Lazarus.
16. He preached on Mars' Hill in Athens.
17. Three thousand persons were saved under his preaching on the day of Pentecost.
18. Saul held the coats of those stoning this young man.
19. An angel let this man out of prison.
20. He was taken by a mob to the edge of a hill, where they planned to push him over the cliff.

Old Testament Persons

Maybe you are more familiar with people in the Old Testament. Try this quiz and see.

1. This wicked queen killed the prophets of Jehovah.
2. Samson shouldn't have trusted this woman.
3. He fell off his chair and broke his neck when he received word the Ark of God had been taken.
4. This prophet told his servant to look toward the sea seven times for rain clouds.
5. A king who was murdered by his servants.
6. This man was a cousin of Saul and captain of his army.
7. A queen who refused to go to her husband when he called for her.
8. A young man who was a very fast runner.
9. Because he was so greedy, this man was stricken with leprosy.
10. A prophetess and judge of Israel.
11. The father of the Hebrew people.
12. A proud man who tried to get all the Jewish people killed.
13. A man who didn't see death; God took him.
14. A preacher who refused to preach in a wicked city.
15. She despised King David when she saw him dancing before the Lord.
16. He was told to take his shoes off because he stood on holy ground.
17. King David remembered his covenant with this man's father and restored all the land of Saul to him.
18. A man who could do unusual things because of his great strength.
19. A young lad hit this man in the forehead with a pebble.
20. She drew water for the camels of Abraham's servant.

Summarize the Books

How many books of the Old Testament can you identify by a brief summary? Some of these may be a little difficult. You're pretty smart if you can get them all.

1. A story of a young widow who showed deep loyalty to her mother-in-law.
2. A long book, it contains a collection of hymns and praises.
3. The laws of sacrifice, purification, and atonement are detailed explicitly in this book.
4. This book is an exhortation to the people to rebuild the temple.
5. If you enjoy reading love stories and songs, you will enjoy reading this book.
6. We can read all about the reign of King David in this book.
7. We learn of the temptation and fall of man in this book.
8. The crossing of the Jordan River and the conquest of Canaan is told here.
9. Forty years of wandering in the wilderness.
10. We learn the story of the life of Samuel and Saul if we read this book.
11. This is the story of a man's suffering and the efforts of his friends to convince him that he is a sinner.
12. This is a story of a wise and devout Hebrew captive at the Babylonian court.
13. This book tells of the coming day of wrath and final redemption.
14. This book is a prophecy of the destruction of Nineveh.
15. A Judean shepherd proclaims God's justice in this book.
16. This book expresses the mourning and repentance of the exiles in Babylon.
17. A story about a prophet who ran away to avoid preaching in a wicked city.

18. This book condemns corrupt worship and life.
19. A story of a beautiful queen who, because of her faith, saved her people.
20. The words of the wise.

Just Kinfolk

Many names in the Bible, like David, Paul, Esther, Luke, are so familiar to us that they could be our relatives. But many of them were relatives. Can you identify the relationship between the pairs of names below?

1. King Saul was Jonathan's __F__.
2. Sarah was Abraham's __W__.
3. Lois was Timothy's __GM__.
4. David was Ruth's _____.
5. Laban was Joseph's _____.
6. Ruth was Orpha's __Sis. L__.
7. Leah was Rachel's __S__.
8. Jethro was Moses' _____.
9. John was James' __B__.
10. Salome was Herodias's __D M__.
11. Hannah was Samuel's __M__.
12. Elisabeth was Mary's __C__.
13. Rehoboam was Solomon's _____.
14. Priscilla was Aquila's __W__.
15. Adam was Abel's __F__.
16. Abraham was Lot's __Unsle__.
17. Esther was Mordecai's __Neice__.
18. David was Saul's __Son in Law__.
19. Andrew was Peter's __B__.
20. Naomi was Ruth's __Min Law__.
21. Timothy was Eunice's __S__.
22. Nun was Joshua's _____.
23. Jacob was Laban's _____.
24. Abel was Cain's __B__.

44

Please Tell Me the Name

Just as we have a first, middle, and a last name, people in the Bible often had "another" name. Can you give the other name that each person below may have answered to?

1. Peter _____
2. Abraham _____
3. Judas _____
4. Mark _____
5. Paul _____
6. Sarah _____
7. Dorcas _____
8. Daniel _____
9. Esther _____
10. Jacob _____
11. John _____
12. Elijah _____
13. Thomas _____
14. Gideon _____
15. Goliath _____
16. Naomi _____
17. Matthew _____
18. Barnabas _____
19. Solomon _____
20. Joseph _____

Their Names Had Meanings

Most of the names in the Bible had meanings and many babies were given a particular name because of the meaning. How many names and their meanings can you match?

1. Moses
2. Samuel
3. Isaac
4. Job
5. Ezekiel
6. Jeremiah
7. Isaiah
8. Dorcas
9. Emmanuel
10. Bethel
11. Exodus
12. Adam
13. Hannah
14. Malachi
15. David
16. Esther
17. Abraham
18. Peter
19. Stephen
20. Golgotha
21. Mara
22. Israel
23. Daniel
24. Martha
25. Hagar

a. God hath heard
b. God with us
c. The Lord gives salvation
d. House of God
e. Drawn out of water
f. Hostile
g. Gazelle

h. Beloved
i. Laughter
j. Flight
k. The Lord exalts
l. Father of a multitude
m. Man
n. Having power with God
o. God strengthens
p. Skull
q. Grace
r. Rock
s. Messenger
t. Bitter
u. God is my judge
v. Star
w. Lady
x. Crown
y. A way out

Explain the Meaning

Jesus taught by using parables to show a particular meaning. Match the parables to the meanings given below.

1. Parable of the Soils
2. Parable of the Tares
3. Parable of the Mustard Seed
4. Parable of the Marriage Feast
5. Parable of the Talents
6. Parable of the Good Samaritan
7. Parable of the Lost Sheep

a. This parable shows that God can make an enormous increase from a meager beginning.
b. The fruitfulness of the Gospel depends upon the attitude and spiritual depth of the hearer.
c. If you use and invest wisely what you are given to do, you will receive greater responsibility; however, if you fail to invest what you have, it will result in condemnation.
d. This parable explains the appearance of evil in the Christian's life and how the kingdom will be purged of all evil.
e. Salvation is offered to many, but only the few who heed it seriously and wear the appropriate attire will be permitted to enter the gate of heaven.
f. Every person is important in the eyes of God.
g. Anyone who stands in need of assistance is my neighbor.

How Did They Travel?

There were some unusual ways of traveling in the Bible, means of transportation we have never used. See if you can guess them.

1. Elijah traveled to heaven in one.
2. These animals were used by men traveling to see the Christ child.
3. This meek animal was used by the poorer people as a means of transportation.
4. In times of war these animals were used because of their swiftness.
5. Paul was traveling in one when it wrecked.
6. Jehu was known to drive one recklessly fast.
7. Because of the dangers along the road, most people traveled in large groups called _____.
8. Mary no doubt rode this animal when traveling to Bethlehem.
9. Cain traveled in this manner when he left home.
10. Abraham's servants traveled a great distance on these animals when seeking a wife for Isaac.
11. Noah traveled to Mount Ararat in one.
12. Jonah traveled a short distance in one.
13. Saul rode in it as a means of escape.
14. An Ethiopian eunuch was reading the Scriptures while riding in one.
15. A man with palsy was carried on one to Jesus.
16. Jesus rode on one into Jerusalem.
17. Absalom was riding on one when he got his hair caught in a tree.
18. Mordecai was paraded through the streets, in honor, on one.
19. Pharaoh sent these to bring Joseph's family to Egypt.

An Alphabet of Cities and Places

It seems as if the names of cities and towns in the Bible were almost as numerous as the names of people. See if you can identify the cities and places listed below. The alphabet letter will help.

1. A _____ Disciples of Christ were first called Christians here.
2. B _____ The town of Jesus' birth.
3. C _____ A city on the shore of the Sea of Galilee.
4. D _____ An ancient city that was the capital of Syria.
5. E _____ A city built by Cain.
6. F _____ A military defense, figurative of God's care.
7. G _____ Most of the apostles were from this place.
8. H _____ The unseen world.
9. I _____ A city of Asia Minor in which Paul preached.
10. J _____ Called the City of David.
11. K _____ A Canaanite city taken by Joshua.
12. L _____ Paul and Barnabas fled to this city from persecution in Iconium.
13. M _____ Paul received in a vision the call to come preach in this city.
14. N _____ The land where Cain went after leaving home.
15. O _____ A town of the Benjamites.
16. P _____ Paul blinded a sorcerer in this city.
17. R _____ The capital of the Roman Empire, Paul desired to preach in this city.
18. S _____ Jesus said he "must needs go through _____."
19. T _____ City of Paul's birth.
20. U _____ The early home of Abraham.
21. V _____ Another name for low-lying ground.
22. W _____ The Israelites wandered here for many years.

From Ashes to Victory

Everyone speaks of the patience of Job. He did go through a lot. How well do you know the story?

1. Job called this land home.
2. The number of children Job had.
3. The number of animals Job owned.
4. He told God, "I've been going to and fro in the earth, and from walking up and down in it."
5. Two adjectives the Lord used to describe Job.
6. The first animals that Job lost.
7. The group of people who stole Job's camels.
8. The one thing God would not permit Satan to do to Job.
9. The first physical problem Satan inflicted on Job.
10. After using a potsherd to scrape himself, Job went and sat down among them.
11. The names of the three friends who came to visit Job.
12. The main purpose of the three friends' visit.
13. The length of time Job's friends sat down with him upon the ground.
14. The old lion perisheth for lack of it.
15. It killeth the foolish man.
16. Job said the weight of his grief and calamity would be heavier than this.
17. Job's flesh was clothed with these two things.
18. Man that is born of woman is full of it.
19. The kind of comforters Job said his friends were.
20. Job said the shadow of it was on his eyelids.
21. At the end of his suffering, Job was blessed with how many children?
22. The number of animals he owned.
23. The name given to Job's first daughter.
24. The number of years Job lived after his suffering.
25. The number of generations he saw in his sons.

Those Sparkling Gems

Sometimes we forget they had precious gems and minerals and stones in Bible times. But the following questions will remind you they were popular then, too.

1. Solomon made his drinking cups from this.
2. The priest had this green-colored gem in his breastplate.
3. A precious stone of a bright-blue color seen in the foundation of the New Jerusalem as seen in John's vision.
4. A sparkling, clear stone in the breastplate.
5. Lot's wife turned into this mineral.
6. This stone is referred to as having a great price.
7. Fire and _____ rained upon Sodom.
8. Ahab's palace was made of this.
9. Jesus was betrayed with thirty pieces of it.
10. The white stone that Mary's ointment box was made of.
11. A gate made of this mineral opened of its own accord for Peter and the angel.
12. This semiprecious, gold-colored stone is associated with Ethiopia.

The Flutter of Angels' Wings

There were a lot of occasions in the Scriptures that angels had a part in. How many incidents of their appearances can you recall?

1. An angel smote the _____ army.
2. _____ was completely surrounded by invisible angels.
3. An angel announced to _____ the coming birth of John the Baptist.
4. Jesus didn't have to die, for He could have called _____ legions of angels. But He chose to die because He loved us.
5. _____ was the patron angel of Judah.
6. Angels were ascending and descending on a ladder in _____ dream.
7. An angel announced to _____ the birth of his son.
8. _____ was led by an angel to send for Peter.
9. _____ wrestled all night with an angel.
10. Angels ministered to _____ during a great temptation.
11. _____ and _____ and _____ are the only three angels mentioned by name in the New Testament.
12. _____ is the archangel.
13. An angel struck _____ dead.
14. _____ angels watch over young children.
15. _____ prepared a meal for an angel.
16. An angel stood by _____ during a great storm.
17. An angel was detained by _____.
18. Angels were the messengers of judgment on _____.
19. Angels promised the return of _____.
20. The angel of the Lord came and touched _____ twice while he slept, awakening him.
21. An angel found _____ by a fountain of water in the wilderness.
22. _____ announced to Mary that she would bear a son.
23. Angels will be the _____ at the end of time.
24. _____ will accompany Christ when He comes again.
25. _____ death was intercepted by an angel.
26. Angels announced the birth of Jesus to _____.

27. _____ angels were sitting in the tomb when Mary Magdalene arrived with her friends on Sunday morning.
28. The devil has _____ angels.
29. An angel arranged the _____ of Isaac and Rebekah.
30. An angel rebuked the Israelites for _____.

So Much Symbolism

A lot of symbolism is used in the Bible. Try to match the meaning above with the symbol below. This one is difficult. You can feel pretty smart if you get all of them.

1. Wedding garment
2. Fire
3. Lost sheep
4. Ashes
5. Pillar of cloud
6. Sprinkled blood
7. Water
8. Oil
9. Passover
10. Wine
11. Fortress
12. Fox
13. Foundation
14. Hyssop
15. Incense
16. Leaven
17. Marrow
18. Nakedness
19. Olive
20. Rainbow
21. Reed
22. Sabbath
23. Dove
24. Dry leaves
25. Sand

a. Divine Presence
b. Cleansing
c. The atoning blood
d. Purity of one's heart and life
e. Atonement
f. Mourning
g. Purifying

h. Covenant
i. Sinners
j. Healing
k. Spiritual poverty
l. The heavens
m. Weakness
n. God's care
o. Spiritual cleansing
p. Holy Spirit
q. Unfaithful prophet
r. Hypocrisy and other evils
s. Rest period
t. An acceptable sacrifice
u. Promise
v. Numberlessness
w. Prosperity
x. Ruin and decay
y. Good things

There's No *A* in *Quiz*

The answers to the following questions all begin with the letter *A*. Does that make it easier?

1. This king was considered the most wicked king that ever lived.
2. A brother of Moses, he was a high priest.
3. She killed her whole family to become queen.
4. One of the three Jews saved from the fiery furnace.
5. This king put to death those who had murdered his father.
6. A title of honor bestowed upon Caesar.
7. Paul preached on Mars' Hill in this city.
8. A woman of understanding and of beauty; upon the death of her husband, she became the wife of David.
9. After Saul spared the life of this king, Samuel killed him.
10. Though eighty-four years old, this woman visited the temple daily and was there when Joseph and Mary brought the baby Jesus to be dedicated.
11. The word used to refer to the announcement by Gabriel to Mary that she was to give birth to the Son of God.
12. In Jesus' life it took place forty days after Easter; it was a bodily disappearance into the sky.

How Many Were There?

How many were involved in the following incidents and situations?

1. The number of Jesus' apostles.
2. The children of Israel marched around the walls of Jericho how many times?
3. Jesus said we must forgive our brother this many times, meaning without limit.
4. This many sheep were in the fold when the Good Shepherd went to find the lost one.
5. Although they probably traveled in a great caravan, we usually think of this number of wise men.
6. After feeding the vast multitude, this number of baskets of unused food was collected.
7. The number of spies Rahab helped.
8. The number of days Jonah spent in the belly of the whale.
9. Noah and his family were in the ark approximately _____.
10. This number of men could be seen walking inside the fiery furnace.
11. Judas betrayed Jesus for _____ pieces of silver.
12. Jehoash was _____ years old when he became king.
13. Daniel prayed _____ times a day.
14. Jacob worked _____ years to get Rachel.
15. Jesus healed _____ lepers.
16. The number of books in the New Testament.
17. The number of books in the Old Testament.
18. The number of camels Abraham's servant took when he went to find a wife for Isaac.
19. Joseph's brothers sold him for this many pieces of silver.
20. The number of lefthanded men in Judges who could sling stones at a hair breadth and not miss.

Tell Me the Author

Do you know the authors of the books of the Bible? A list of books and authors has been given. Try to match the book to its author. The authors may be used several times.

1. Psalms
2. Jude
3. Philemon
4. Matthew
5. Genesis
6. Leviticus
7. Acts
8. Haggai
9. Revelation
10. Isaiah
11. Exodus
12. Proverbs
13. Luke
14. Titus
15. Micah
16. Joel
17. 1 Timothy
18. Ephesians
19. Galatians
20. 1 John
21. Numbers
22. Jonah
23. Ecclesiastes
24. Romans
25. Song of Solomon

a. Moses
b. John
c. Paul
d. David
e. Jude
f. Solomon
g. James

h. Luke
 i. Isaiah
 j. Matthew
k. Joel
 l. Haggai
m. Micah
 n. Jonah

Water, Water, Water

Many important events in the Bible center around water. See how many you can match. The answers may be used more than once.

1. God caused this body of water to divide.
2. Moses struck this to get water.
3. A blind man washed his eyes here.
4. Abram received all the land from the river of Egypt to this river.
5. Jesus crossed this brook the night of His betrayal.
6. Jesus turned water into wine here.
7. Elijah was fed by ravens at this brook.
8. John baptized Jesus in this river.
9. Naaman dipped seven times in this river and was healed of leprosy.
10. The head of an ax fell into this river.
11. Jonah left from this port when going to sea.
12. Moses was placed on this river in a basket.
13. A harp-shaped body of water.
14. Jesus commanded the storm on this sea to quiet.
15. David said he watered it with his tears.
16. They water the earth.
17. God waters them from His chambers.
18. Peter walked on this body of water.
19. The waters of this country were turned to blood.
20. Another name for the Dead Sea.
21. The Mediterranean Sea is called this.
22. Ezra proclaimed a fast at this river.
23. Ezekiel saw visions of God by this river.
24. A river flowing through the Garden of Eden.
25. Four angels were bound by this river.

a. Cedron
b. Joppa
c. Red Sea
d. Nile
e. Siloam

f. Jordan
g. Cherith
h. Sea of Galilee
i. Rock
j. Euphrates
k. Cana
l. Couch
m. Egypt
n. Hills
o. Showers
p. Salt Sea
q. Chebar
r. Great Sea
s. Pison
t. Ahava

Just Hair

Some Bible passages make reference to a person's hair. Match the name below with a clue above. Some names may be used more than once.

1. My strength was in my hair.
2. I said, "The hairs on your head are numbered."
3. I dried Jesus' feet with my hair.
4. I lost my strength after a haircut.
5. I caught my long hair in a tree.
6. Members of this religious group vowed never to cut their hair.
7. I said a woman's hair is her glory.
8. This man had almost no hair at all.
9. This man had gray hair.
10. He had his hair cut and weighed each year.
11. This man was covered with hair.

a. Jesus
b. Absalom
c. Nazarites
d. Samson
e. Jacob
f. Mary Magdalene
g. Esau
h. Elisha
i. Paul

Blessed Are They

The Psalms call many blessed. See how many verses you can complete.

1. Blessed is the man whose delight is in the _____ of the Lord.
2. Blessed are they that keep _____.
3. Blessed is the man whom thou dost _____, O Lord.
4. Blessed are they who _____ in thy house.
5. Blessed is the man whose _____ is in thee.
6. Blessed is he who considers the _____.
7. Blessed is the man who makes the Lord his _____.
8. Blessed is the man whose transgression is _____.
9. Blessed is the nation whose God is the _____.
10. Blessed is the man to whom the Lord imputes no _____.
11. Blessed is he whom thou dost choose to dwell in thy _____.
12. Blessed is he that cometh in the _____ of the Lord.
13. Blessed are they that keep his _____.
14. Blessed is the man who walketh not in the counsel of the _____.
15. Blessed is every one that _____ the Lord, that walketh in his ways.
16. Blessed is the man whom thou _____.
17. Blessed are the people that know the _____ sound.
18. Blessed are the _____ in the way.
19. Blessed is the man that _____ in him.
20. Blessed are all they who put their _____ in him.

Biblical Facts That Are Nice to Know

How many details about the Bible do you really know? Maybe these facts aren't so important, but they're nice to know. Quick, how many do you know right off?

1. Name the two divisions of the Bible.
2. Number of books in the Old Testament.
3. Number of books in the New Testament.
4. Number of books in the whole Bible.
5. The Old Testament is divided into five divisions. Name them.
6. The New Testment is divided into five divisions. Name them.
7. What is another name for the book of Revelation?
8. In what language was the New Testament written?
9. What books tell you about Christ?
10. What book tells you about the early church?
11. What book tells you about the end of the world and judgment?
12. Name the middle verse of the Bible.
13. What is the longest book of the Bible?
14. What is the longest verse in the Bible?
15. Where is the shortest verse in the Bible?
16. Where is the shortest chapter?
17. Where is the longest chapter?
18. What is the middle book of the Bible?
19. Which two chapters are alike?
20. How many chapters are in the entire Bible?

They Performed Miracles

Jesus wasn't the only person in the Bible God used to perform miracles. Can you name the persons who performed the miracles listed below?

1. Healed Saul's blinded eyes.
2. Raised Dorcas from the dead.
3. Parted the Red Sea.
4. Caused Zacharias to lose his voice.
5. Replenished the widow's meal and oil each day.
6. Caused the moon and sun to stand still.
7. Calmed the Sea of Galilee.
8. Caused an ax head to float.
9. Blinded Elymas, the sorcerer.
10. Turned a rod into a serpent.
11. Raised the Shunammite's son.
12. Saw chariots of fire on the mountain.
13. Replaced a servant's ear.
14. Healed a lame beggar at the gate called Beautiful.
15. Healed Peter's mother-in-law.
16. Released Peter from prison.
17. Healed a slave girl.
18. The fall of Jericho.
19. Divided the Jordan River.
20. Cured a lame man.
21. Turned water into wine.
22. Cured Naaman of leprosy.
23. He shook a viper off his hand.
24. Restored a withered hand.
25. Opened the eyes of a man born blind.

Identify the Word

Each word below is the name of a mountain, body of water, a town, or a garden (see the listing on the next page). It's up to you to identify them.

1. Ararat
2. Jordan
3. Hermon
4. Macedonia
5. Gilboa
6. Ziklag
7. Nebo
8. Nazareth
9. Tekoa
10. Nob
11. Tabor
12. Mediterranean
13. Sinai
14. Black
15. Caspian
16. Nineveh
17. Antioch
18. Euphrates
19. Red
20. Ebal
21. Damascus
22. Tigris
23. Gerizim
24. Joppa
25. Persian
26. Shiloh
27. Bethel
28. Carmel
29. Lycia
30. Eden
31. Gerar
32. Berea
33. Ephraim

34. Zion
35. Gethsemane

a. Mountain
b. Body of water
c. Town
d. Garden

Scriptural Anatomy

Many stories in the Bible center around certain parts of the anatomy. Can you name these parts?

1. The part of our anatomy that God looks upon.
2. If it offends thee, pluck it out.
3. Jesus washed them on His disciples to show the spirit of humility.
4. Stephen told the Sanhedrin that theirs were stiff.
5. It was often shaven when vows were taken.
6. Solomon said a sound one is the life of the flesh.
7. Eli fell from a chair and broke it.
8. Goliath had twenty-four of them.
9. A particular generation had some like swords.
10. David prayed for God to create within him a clean one.
11. Mephibosheth was dropped by his nurse and injured them.
12. Samson had his gouged out by the Philistines.
13. Jacob had this part of his body dislocated as he wrestled with the angel.
14. Malchus had it severed from his body by Peter's sword in the Garden of Gethsemane.
15. A viper attached itself to this part of Paul's body.
16. David severed this part of Goliath's body.
17. Jesus restored this part of a man's body that was withered.
18. Referred to as a house of clay.
19. As He hung upon the cross, the soldier pierced this part of Jesus' body.
20. This part of your body shall live forever.
21. Herodias's daughter asked for this part of John the Baptist on a platter.
22. Moses wasn't permitted to see this part of God.
23. This part of Samson's body created a lot of problems for him.
24. Moses had leprosy on this part of his body.
25. God breathed life into this part of Adam's body.
26. James said this member of our body could cause a lot of trouble.

27. Moses was permitted to see this part of God.
28. If someone slaps it, turn it and let the opposite one be slapped, too.

Similes in the Proverbs

Many characteristics in the Bible have been likened unto something else. Can you combine phrases from each column to make one complete phrase?

1. A virtuous woman is as
2. The hoary head is as
3. The folly of fools is as
4. A merry heart is as
5. The path of the just is as
6. The way of the wicked is
7. The king's wrath is as
8. A word fitly spoken is like
9. The king's favor is as
10. A contentious woman is as a
11. Good news from a far country is as
12. Jealousy is as
13. The fruit of the righteous is as
14. A fair woman without discretion is as
15. The fear of the Lord is as
16. The words of a man's mouth are as
17. The wellspring of wisdom is as
18. Bread of deceit is as
19. The mouth of a strange woman is as
20. A wise reprover upon an obedient ear is as
21. Bread eaten in secret is as
22. He that is slow to anger is
23. He that hath no rule over his spirit is as
24. The man that beareth false witness against his neighbor is as
25. A faithful messenger to them that send him is as

a. a crown of glory
b. deceit
c. cold waters to a thirsty soul
d. like darkness
e. apples of gold in pictures of silver
f. better than the mighty

g. a city ... broken down
h. a crown to her husband
i. continual dripping on a rainy day
j. deep waters
k. dew upon the grass
l. a flowing brook
m. a good medicine
n. an earring of gold
o. the rage of a man
p. a deep pit
q. the roaring of a lion
r. the beginning of wisdom
s. a pleasant thing
t. a shining light
u. snow in the time of harvest
v. a tree of life
w. a sweetness to a man
x. a maul, a sword, and a sharp arrow
y. a jewel of gold in a swine's snout.

Admonishments to Heed

Many Scripture verses give us bits of admonishment we ought to obey. Match them up and see if you obey them.

1. Make no friendship with a man given to _____.
2. Remember now thy Creator in the days of thy _____.
3. In all thy ways acknowledge him and he shall _____ thy paths.
4. _____ to show thyself approved unto God.
5. _____ without ceasing.
6. _____ in the Lord with all thine heart; and lean not unto thine own understanding.
7. They that wait upon the Lord shall renew their _____.
8. Rebuke not an _____.
9. A new commandment I give you, that ye _____ one another.
10. Men ought always to pray and not to _____.
11. Let not mercy and _____ forsake thee.
12. Let your _____ shine before men.
13. Judge not, that ye be not _____.
14. Take ye heed, _____ and pray: for ye know not when the time is.
15. Be _____ in the Lord.
16. Let not the sun go down upon your _____.
17. Let no corrupt _____ proceed out of your mouth.
18. In everything give _____.
19. Set your _____ on things above.
20. Confess your _____ one to another.

a. Youth
b. Judged
c. Strength
d. Anger
e. Watch
f. Elder
g. Study
h. Faint
i. Faults

j. Affection
k. Direct
l. Truth
m. Pray
n. Light
o. Strong
p. Trust
q. Wrath
r. Thanks
s. Communication
t. Love

From Shepherd to King

The shepherd boy who became king is a story known to everyone. You may know the story, but this quiz may be difficult. Try it anyway.

1. The name of David's father.
2. God sent this prophet to Bethlehem to anoint David king.
3. David was one of how many sons?
4. The number of days Goliath presented himself to King Saul's army.
5. While watching his flocks, David once fought off these two animals.
6. David chose five smooth stones from out of this place.
7. How many of the five stones did it take to kill Goliath?
8. David's friendship with this man has become a classic example of true friendship.
9. The number of times Saul hurled his javelin at David.
10. The daughter King Saul gave to David for a wife.
11. After escaping through the window, David fled to this man.
12. Jonathan made this with the house of David.
13. The number of men Saul took with him to look for David.
14. The wife of Nabal, who showed kindness to David and his men.
15. The town Achish gave to David and his men to live in.
16. The beautiful woman whom David saw bathing herself.
17. David had this man sent to the front lines of the hottest battle so that he might be killed.
18. The prophet God sent to warn David because of his sin.
19. The mother of David's son, Solomon.
20. David asked for Zadok, the priest, Nathan, the prophet, and Benaiah to anoint this son as king.

The Name, Sir? 'Tis Paul

We look at Saul with contempt and at Paul with love, yet they are the same man. His life is a testimony to what God can do with a person who is committed to Him.

1. The first time we see Saul is at the stoning of this man.
2. A great persecution was being waged against the church here.
3. Those of the church were scattering into these regions.
4. Saul received letters from the high priest to bring back people who had escaped to this city.
5. After being blinded, Saul was led to Damascus to a house on this street.
6. God instructed this disciple to go and pray with Saul.
7. The disciples helped Saul to escape from them by letting him down over the city wall in a basket.
8. This man was sent with Paul on his first missionary journey.
9. Another name given to Paul by the people in Lystra.
10. Jews from these two cities stoned Paul and drew him out of the city.
11. Barnabas departed from Paul because this young man wasn't permitted to travel with them.
12. Paul chose this man to accompany him on his second missionary trip.
13. A woman in Thyatira who opened her home to Paul.
14. A young man who became as a son to Paul.
15. He fell asleep under Paul's long preaching and fell out the window and died.
16. The number of persons on Paul's ship when it wrecked.
17. After their ship wrecked, the passengers escaped to this island.
18. What was the weather like when Paul and his fellow passengers arrived on the island?
19. A very venomous one came out of the heat of burning sticks and fastened itself onto Paul's hand.
20. The chief man of the island of Melita.
21. Paul called himself a prisoner of Jesus Christ for whom?

22. A man to whom Paul wrote in behalf of his runaway slave.
23. A runaway slave who became a Christian.
24. Paul asked Philemon to receive his slave not as a slave, but as a _____.
25. The reason Paul knew he could write to Philemon.

Principal Thoughts

Many books in the Bible have a principal thought or subject. Name the book that has the principal thought or subject listed below. Most of the books are used. Don't give up; keep chugging.

1. Problem of suffering
2. The division of the kingdom
3. The reign of David
4. An errand of mercy to Nineveh
5. The founding of the Hebrew nation
6. The laws of the Hebrew nation
7. The rebuilding of Jerusalem
8. The conquest of Canaan
9. The national hymnbook of Israel
10. The messianic prophet
11. The escape of Israel from being exterminated
12. The prophecy of the age of the Holy Spirit
13. The destruction of the city of Nineveh
14. Jesus the Messiah
15. The formation of the church
16. The deity of Jesus
17. Jesus the Wonderful
18. The Lord's Second Coming
19. Jesus the Son of Man
20. Jesus the Son of God
21. The conversion of a runaway slave
22. The ultimate triumph of Christ
23. The nature of Christ's work
24. Good works
25. Salvation by grace, not by law

Complete the Scripture

The Scripture verses below are rather short and are easily separated. Match the beginning of the verses in the first section to their endings in the second section.

1. Take my yoke upon you
2. Repent and be baptized
3. Fear God
4. Resist the devil
5. Behold the Lamb of God
6. Though your sins be as scarlet
7. Be not deceived
8. Remember the sabbath day
9. It is more blessed to give
10. Be sure your sin
11. Son of man
12. God is our refuge and strength
13. A soft answer
14. Pride goeth before destruction
15. For the wages of sin is death
16. Be thou faithful unto death
17. Him that cometh to me
18. He that loveth pleasure
19. Woe unto them
20. I am a rose of Sharon

a. and he will flee from you.
b. they shall be as white as snow.
c. and I will give thee the crown of life.
d. and learn of me.
e. God is not mocked.
f. a very present help in trouble.
g. I will in no wise cast out.
h. every one of you.
i. can these bones live?
j. shall be a poor man.
k. turneth away wrath.
l. and keep his commandments.

m. will find you out.
n. but the gift of God is eternal life through Jesus Christ
   our Lord.
o. to keep it holy.
p. that rise up early in the morning.
q. and a haughty spirit before a fall.
r. than to receive.
s. a lily of the valleys.
t. which taketh away the sin of the world.

And the Songwriter Is . . .

Some of the songs we sing in church today are very old, and we know them almost by heart. But do you know who wrote those songs? Five songwriters are well-known. Match the songs below with the person who wrote it, listed on the next page.

1. Near the Cross
2. O for a Thousand Tongues
3. To God Be the Glory
4. At the Cross
5. Jesus Is Calling
6. Christ, the Lord, Is Risen Today
7. Out of the Depths I Cry to Thee
8. Hark! The Herald Angels Sing
9. Am I a Soldier of the Cross?
10. From All That Dwell Below the Skies
11. Close to Thee
12. We're Marching to Zion
13. We Will Stand the Storm
14. He Hideth My Soul
15. To the Work
16. Soldiers of Christ, Arise
17. I'll Be a Soldier for Jesus
18. Redeemed
19. Blessed Assurance
20. He Loves Me
21. Jesus, Thine All-victorious Love
22. Jesus, Lover of My Soul
23. A Mighty Fortress Is Our God
24. Love Divine
25. When I Survey
26. Come Thou Long-expected Jesus
27. Saved by Grace
28. My Saviour First of All
29. Jesus Shall Reign
30. I Am Thine, O Lord

a. John Wesley
b. Fanny Crosby
c. Isaac Watts
d. Charles Wesley
e. Martin Luther

Winged Insects

Those little, tiny bugs. Yes, they were around in Bible days, too. See if you can identify the little things given in the clues below.

1. John the Baptist ate them in the wilderness.
2. These were sent by God to drive out the Hivites, Canaanites and Hittites.
3. Jesus said the Pharisees would strain at one of these and swallow a camel.
4. We should consider the industry of them and be wise.
5. Aaron was instructed to stretch out his rod and smite the dust of the land so it would become as _____ throughout the land of Egypt.
6. One buildeth his house as one of these.
7. A hypocrite's trust shall be this.
8. The fourth plague on Egypt—they came in swarms.
9. David said that all the nations compassed him about like these.
10. Dead ones cause the ointment of the apothecary to smell badly.
11. The Midianites with all of their cattle and camels resembled these because they were without number.
12. David asked King Saul if he were pursuing a dog or one of these.

What's In a *B?*

Each answer below begins with the letter *B*. It may be a person, place, or thing. Can you decide?

1. He purchased Ruth after he took his shoes off.
2. After selling his property, he laid the money at the apostles' feet.
3. It was grown in Joab's field.
4. Jesus healed a man by this pool and told him to take up his bed and walk.
5. Be careful if you take her young from her, for she becomes very mean.
6. An angel asked this man why he had struck his mule.
7. They captured the Jews, then told them to sing happy songs.
8. Joseph placed a silver cup into this brother's sack of grain.
9. The name of a container.
10. An officer of Herod's.
11. An item used often in building.
12. A word used to mean "crooked paths."
13. A friend of Job's.
14. You would find this piece on a bridle.
15. God created them on the fifth day.
16. Jesus fed 5,000 people near here.
17. The king of Sodom in Abraham's day.
18. Jesus made His triumphal entry into Jerusalem on a colt obtained from here.
19. The apostle James was executed by this method.
20. This is to be administered in the name of the Father, the Son, and the Holy Ghost.
21. Pilate released this man rather than Jesus.
22. Another name for a medicinal balsam.
23. It was called the land of the Chaldeans.
24. A prince of Judah.
25. The son of Jacob by Rachel.
26. She was a daughter of Agrippa.
27. Referred to as the staff of life.
28. Something made by churning.

Which One?

Would you have found James, Zacchaeus, or Thomas up in the sycamore tree? If you said Zacchaeus, you're right. Can you do as well with the questions below?

1. Jacob was deceived by him.
    a. Joseph b. Isaac c. Laban
2. The first plague on Egypt.
    a. locusts b. blood c. flies
3. Aaron's firstborn son.
    a. Abihu b. Eleazar c. Nadab
4. A queen who refused to go to her husband when summoned.
    a. Vashti b. Esther c. Bernice
5. Jesus was visited by this man during the night.
    a. Jairus b. Nicodemus c. Zacchaeus
6. Joel was the son of this man.
    a. Eli b. Pethuel c. Zeboim
7. The famine in the days of David lasted this number of years.
    a. three years b. seven years c. five years
8. Samuel was buried at his house here.
    a. Joppa b. Chaldea c. Ramah
9. Sarah's age when she died.
    a. 120 years b. 127 years c. 135 years
10. He hid prophets in a cave and fed them bread and water.
    a. Nahum b. Obadiah c. Hosea
11. The king who married Mordecai's cousin.
    a. Ahasuerus b. Haman c. Hammedatha
12. The man chosen to take the place of Judas among the disciples.
    a. Matthias b. Joseph c. Barsabas
13. Paul asked for the cloak he had left at Troas with this man.
    a. Alexander b. Carpus c. Eubulus
14. Paul caused blindness to come upon this sorcerer.
    a. Elymas b. Paulus c. Simeon

15. Moses' sons were named in this tribe.
    a. Judah b. Dan c. Levi
16. A queen who gave King Solomon an IQ test.
    a. Esther b. Sheba c. Jezebel
17. On this day God created the fowl of the air, the whales of the sea, and every living creature that moveth.
    a. second b. fourth c. fifth
18. This man found grace in the eyes of the Lord.
    a. Enoch b. Noah c. Abraham
19. Joseph's brother who delivered him from death.
    a. Judah b. Zebulun c. Reuben
20. Joseph was sold to the Ishmaelites for how many pieces of silver?
    a. twenty b. thirty c. forty
21. Paul received a message in a dream to go here to preach.
    a. Cornith b. Rome c. Macedonia
22. This is the substance of things hoped for.
    a. faith b. hope c. charity
23. The high priest at the time of Jesus' trial.
    a. Pilate b. Caiaphas c. Herod
24. The number of the chariots of God.
    a. 20,000 b. 30,000 c. 40,000
25. Jonah tried to flee from the presence of God by going to this city.
    a. Joppa b. Tarshish c. Nineveh
26. The first of Saul's sons to be killed by the Philistines.
    a. Jonathan b. Abinadab c. Malchishua
27. He prayed for water to quench his thirst.
    a. Samson b. Elijah c. Nahum
28. This man was a silversmith by trade.
    a. Titus b. Erastus c. Demetrius
29. This church was rebuked for its lukewarmness.
    a. Rome b. Laodicea c. Corinth
30. Another name for Dorcas.
    a. Tabitha b. Hadassah c. Abigail

Name the Mary

There were several Marys named in the New Testament. Sometimes it's difficult to keep them separate. Which Mary does each clue below fit?

1. Jesus cast seven demons out of this Mary.
2. She anointed Jesus' feet with costly perfume and wiped them with her hair.
3. This Mary was a kinswoman of the mother of John the Baptist.
4. A group of Christians met in her home to pray for the release of Peter from prison.
5. After finding the stone had been rolled away from the tomb, she quickly ran and told Peter and John the body of Jesus had been taken away.
6. She sat at Jesus' feet and listened to Him eagerly when He visited at her home.
7. She had a maid named Rhoda.
8. She attended the yearly passover with her husband.
9. This Mary had a brother named Barnabas.
10. After His resurrection, Jesus made His first appearance to her.
11. She became one of Jesus' most devoted disciples.
12. Jesus raised her brother from the dead, after he had been dead for four days.
13. She received a stern rebuke from Jesus at a wedding in Cana.
14. At the cross Jesus handed this woman into the care of John.
15. This Mary was rebuked by her sister for not helping with household duties.

a. Virgin Mary
b. Mary Magdalene
c. Mary of Bethany
d. Mary, mother of Mark

Jesus' Sermon on the Mount

Jesus preached the greatest sermon that has ever been preached. Multitudes heard it. Have you read it? Answer the questions below and see how much of His sermon you remember.

1. Whosoever is angry with his brother without a cause shall be in danger of it.
2. He that looks on a woman to lust after her has committed it in his heart.
3. Heaven is God's _____.
4. Earth is God's _____.
5. You shall not swear by these, because you cannot make a one of them black or white.
6. If a man sues you and takes away your coat, then give him this, too.
7. You should love them, as well as your neighbor.
8. You must bless those that do this to you.
9. This must be given to those who hate you.
10. If someone despitefully uses you, _____ for him.
11. Your Father in heaven causes this to rise on the evil and good.
12. This is sent by the Father on the just and unjust.
13. They disfigure their faces when they fast.
14. No man can serve two of them.
15. They don't sow, reap or gather into barns, yet the Father feedeth them.
16. Even Solomon in all his glory was not arrayed as one of these.
17. Seek this first, along with God's righteousness.
18. You will see much more clearly if this is taken out of your eye.
19. Don't cast them before swine, because they will be trampled.
20. The gate is _____ and the way is _____ that leadeth to destruction.
21. The gate to heaven is _____ and the way is _____.
22. Don't listen to them, because they come in sheep's clothing and are ravening wolves on the inside.

23. You shall know men by their _____.
24. A wise man will build his house upon this.
25. The foolish man built his house upon this.

Who Was Called?

Some people in the Bible can be identified by what they were called. Can you guess who each phrase below identifies?

1. The beloved physician.
2. The sons of thunder.
3. The friend of God.
4. The man after God's own heart.
5. The man whose eyes were open.
6. The supplanter.
7. The meekest of all men.
8. A good man, full of the Holy Spirit and of faith.
9. The sweet psalmist of Israel.
10. The doubter.
11. The rock.
12. The betrayer.
13. The virgin mother.
14. The mighty man of valor.
15. The weeping prophet.
16. The beloved disciple.
17. The first Christian martyr.
18. The father of Christian church history.
19. A fugitive and vagabond.
20. The prophet of the people.

A Bit of Everything

Read each of the following questions and see how many you know.

1. His nurse dropped him when he was five years old, and he became lame in both feet.
2. This man was caught and hanged in an oak tree.
3. He walked with God and was not, for God took him.
4. She became a leper for complaining about Moses.
5. She drew water for the camels of Abraham's servants.
6. A fat man who fell off his chair and broke his neck.
7. This man had an excessive amount of hair covering his body.
8. He was a doctor by profession.
9. He was banished to the Isle of Patmos for preaching.
10. The first apostle to be martyred.
11. The first woman to wear a bridal veil.
12. He had 700 wives.
13. She was thrown out the window, into the street, and eaten by dogs.
14. Peter cut his ear off.
15. He was appointed as chief of the disciples.
16. This handsome king had a ruddy complexion.
17. He will be with Christ at His Second Coming.
18. He called fire down from heaven.
19. A king who committed suicide by falling on his sword.
20. This man was stoned for looting.

Fifty Questions About Jesus

Jesus lived on earth for thirty-three years. Only as we know Him better can we serve Him better. How many questions below can you answer? The questions are not in chronological order.

1. In a dream the angel instructed Joseph to call the child by this name.
2. Jesus called this woman "mother."
3. He was king of Judea at the time of Jesus' birth.
4. Joseph was instructed to take his family to this country to get away from Herod.
5. The wise men followed it as they traveled from the East.
6. This man reigned in Judea after Herod's death.
7. Joseph settled his little family here.
8. A cousin of Jesus, he preached the baptism of repentance for the remission of sins.
9. The number of days Jesus spent in the wilderness.
10. Man can only baptize with water, but Jesus baptizes with this.
11. God sent His Spirit in this form at Jesus' baptism.
12. The number of apostles Jesus called to follow Him.
13. Jesus' Sermon on the Mount begins with nine short virtues of a happy person, which are called the _____.
14. The town of Jesus' birth.
15. A king who asked the wise men to inform him when they had found the Christ child.
16. Jesus performed His first miracle in this town, thus beginning His public ministry.
17. Jesus' disciple who walked on the water to meet Him.
18. This man was released instead of Jesus.
19. Jesus anointed a blind man's eyes with clay and told him to go wash in this pool.
20. The number of fishes the disciples caught after Jesus told them to cast their net on the right side of the ship.
21. Although the crowd said she was dead, Jesus said this man's little girl was only asleep.

22. Moses said there were ten commandments, but Jesus said there were _____.
23. Jesus said His house would be called this.
24. In this town Jesus was anointed for His burial.
25. The Roman governor who was ruling at the time of Jesus' trial.
26. By this well Jesus offered living water to a thirsting woman.
27. In whose name did Jesus say He had come?
28. The kind of bread the small lad had, which Jesus blessed and gave to the multitude.
29. Jesus said He came as this into the world.
30. The form of punishment Pilate subjected Jesus to in trying to appease the crowd.
31. The first temptation Satan subjected Jesus to in the wilderness.
32. To show the depth of His love and concern for us, Jesus said that even these are numbered.
33. The name the prophets said Jesus would be called.
34. The town where Jesus and His disciples ate the passover feast.
35. Jesus and His disciples did this just before going to the Garden of Gethsemane.
36. This man was compelled to carry the cross for Jesus.
37. The man for whom Jesus was thought to have been calling when He cried, "Eloi."
38. The purpose of the women's visit to Jesus' tomb on the sabbath.
39. The second gift the wise men presented to Jesus.
40. The three disciples Jesus took with Him to the Mount of Transfiguration.
41. Two men appearing with Jesus and talking with Him during His transfiguration.
42. This group of people tried to trick Jesus with a Roman coin.
43. Seeing through their trickery of the Roman coin, Jesus called these people _____.
44. This group of people tried to trick Jesus with a question concerning the resurrection, in which they did not believe.

45. Herod, upon hearing of Jesus, thought He was this man risen from the dead.
46. Two miracles the people acknowledged Jesus had performed.
47. The first man Jesus rebuked for sleeping while He was praying in the garden.
48. Peter denied Jesus before the cock crowed this many times.
49. In the temple it was rent in twain from the top to the bottom.
50. Jesus ascended into heaven from a hilltop in this city.

An Alphabet Quiz

This quiz is easy. Each answer begins with the given letter of the alphabet.

1. A _____ A high priest during Moses' time.
2. B _____ Town of Jesus' birth.
3. C _____ Jesus performed His first miracle here.
4. D _____ A young shepherd who later became king.
5. E _____ This man didn't die, for God took him.
6. F _____ Jesus cursed it because it bore no fruit.
7. G _____ Jesus was crucified on this hill.
8. H _____ Abraham's concubine; mother of Ishmael.
9. I _____ Promised son of Abraham and Sarah.
10. J _____ Jesus went to this city for the passover feast.
11. K _____ Saul was the first one of Israel.
12. L _____ The cedars for Solomon's temple came from here.
13. M _____ This apostle had sat at the receipt of customs.
14. N _____ He came to Jesus during the night.
15. O _____ A runaway slave.
16. P _____ John was exiled on this island.
17. Q _____ The position held by Esther.
18. R _____ She worked in the fields of Boaz.
19. S _____ Jesus said, "I must needs go through _____."
20. T _____ A very young man who helped Paul.
21. U _____ A king who died a leper.
22. V _____ It was rent in twain at Jesus' death.
23. W _____ Jesus was tempted three times by Satan here.
24. X _____ A king mentioned in Ezra.
25. Z _____ He climbed a tree to see Jesus.

Find the Verse

Some verses in the Bible are so well-known that you can identify the Scripture reference immediately. Can you match the verses below with their references?

1. The Lord is my shepherd; I shall not want.
2. In all thy ways acknowledge him, and he shall direct thy paths.
3. I have fought a good fight, I have finished my course, I have kept the faith.
4. Make a joyful noise unto the Lord, all ye lands.
5. For all have sinned, and come short of the glory of God.
6. If we confess our sins, he is faithful and just to forgive us our sins, and to cleanse us from all unrighteousness.
7. Let not your heart be troubled: ye believe in God, believe also in me.
8. In my Father's house are many mansions: if it were not so, I would have told you. I go to prepare a place for you.
9. I am the way, the truth and the life: no man cometh unto the Father, but by me.
10. O death, where is thy sting? O grave, where is thy victory?
11. For to me to live is Christ, and to die is gain.
12. I press toward the mark for the prize of the high calling of God in Christ Jesus.
13. Let us therefore come boldly unto the throne of grace, that we may obtain mercy, and find grace to help in time of need.
14. For God so loved the world, that he gave his only begotten Son, that whosoever believeth in him should not perish, but have everlasting life.
15. Bless the Lord, O my soul: and all that is within me, bless his holy name.

a. 2 Timothy 4:7
b. Psalms 103:1

c. Romans 3:23
d. Proverbs 3:6
e. 1 Corinthians 15:55
f. 1 John 1:9
g. Philippians 3:14
h. Psalms 23:1
 i. John 14:2
 j. John 3:16
k. Psalms 100:1
 l. John 14:6
m. Philippians 1:21
n. John 14:1
o. Hebrews 4:16

Where, Oh, Where

Can you name the place the following events took place? It may be in a city, on a mountain, on a body of water, or in a garden.

1. Jonah didn't want to preach in this city.
2. Jesus attended a wedding reception here.
3. King Solomon was visited by the queen from this country.
4. Every member of the house of David had to pay his taxes here.
5. Jesus' triumphal entry was into this city.
6. The first home of Adam and Eve.
7. Jacob lay on the ground, pillowed his head on stones and went to sleep near this town.
8. A little basket floated among the bulrushes on this river.
9. Naomi and Ruth returned to Bethlehem from this country.
10. God showed Moses the Promised Land from the top of this mountain.
11. While in exile on this island, John wrote the book of Revelation.
12. Jesus prayed in the Garden of Gethsemane, at the foot of this mountain.
13. Jesus said He would have gathered together the children of this city as a hen gathered her chicks.
14. This sea is also called Gennesaret.
15. Lot's wife turned into a pillar of salt when she looked back to these.
16. From this place, Jacob chose a bride.
17. In this land, they built a tower that was to reach unto heaven.
18. Elkanah worshiped and offered sacrifices to his Lord yearly at the temple here.
19. Isaiah's vision concerned this country and city.
20. This city in Palestine supplied the Ammonites with soldiers to fight against David.

21. You would find Jacob's well here.
22. This was the home of the witch Saul consulted.
23. Joseph found his brothers feeding their sheep here.
24. Jonah left on a ship to Tarshish from this city.
25. Goliath lived in this town.
26. David fought and killed the great giant here.
27. Paul escaped from this city in a basket.
28. Peter raised Dorcas to life in this city.
29. Jesus was crucified at this place, located just outside Jerusalem.
30. A fortress to which 600 Benjamites fled after escaping slaughter.
31. Jesus went to this city after John the Baptist was thrown into prison.
32. Trumpets and shouting people made the walls of this city collapse.
33. After being sold into this country, Joseph became governor of it.
34. You would have gone to this city if you had wanted to hear Paul preach on Mars' Hill.
35. Jesus' disciples tarried in this city until they were filled with the Holy Spirit.

Alpha

The word *alpha* means "the beginning." Each phrase below starts the first verse of a book in the Bible. Name the book. No help is given.

1. Blessed is the man that walketh not in the counsel of the ungodly.
2. The book of the generation of Jesus Christ, the son of David.
3. The elder unto the elect lady and her children.
4. In the beginning God created the heaven and the earth.
5. Adam, Sheth, Enosh.
6. These be the words which Moses spake unto all Israel.
7. Now King David was old and stricken in years.
8. God, who at sundry times and in divers manners spake in time past.
9. The former treatise have I made, O Theophilus.
10. In the third year of the reign of Jehoiakim.
11. The words of the Preacher, the son of David, king in Jerusalem.
12. There was a man in the land of Uz.
13. Then Moab rebelled against Israel after the death of Ahab.
14. In the beginning was the Word.
15. Now these are the names of the children of Israel.
16. The beginning of the gospel of Jesus Christ, the Son of God.
17. Forasmuch as many have taken in hand to set forth in order a declaration.
18. And the Lord spake unto Moses in the wilderness.

Omega

The word *omega* means "the end." Here are the beginnings of the last verse of thirty books of the Bible. Name the book each verse below ends. This quiz is more difficult than "Alpha."

1. In those days there was no king in Israel.
2. There is no healing of thy bruise; thy wound is grievous.
3. Let every thing that hath breath praise the Lord.
4. The grace of our Lord Jesus Christ be with you all. Amen.
5. And David built there an altar unto the Lord, and offered burnt offerings and peace offerings.
6. For the cloud of the Lord was upon the tabernacle by day, and fire was on it by night.
7. So Joseph died, being an hundred and ten years old.
8. Who is wise, and he shall understand these things?
9. But thou hast utterly rejected us; thou art very wroth against us.
10. And they shall go forth, and look upon the carcases of the men that have transgressed against me.
11. And there are also many other things which Jesus did.
12. Give her of the fruit of her hands; and let her own works praise her in the gates.
13. For Mordecai the Jew was next unto king Ahasuerus.
14. All these had taken strange wives: and some of them had wives by whom they had children.
15. With all his reign and his might, and the times that went over him, and over Israel.
16. Make haste, my beloved, and be thou like to a roe or to a young hart upon the mountains of spices.
17. Thus saith Cyrus king of Persia, All the kingdoms of the earth hath the Lord God of heaven given me.
18. These are the commandments and the judgments, which the Lord commanded by the hand of Moses.
19. It was round about eighteen thousand measures.
20. Preaching the kingdom of God, and teaching those things which concern the Lord Jesus Christ.

21. Let him know, that he which converteth the sinner from the error of his way shall save a soul from death.
22. Little children, keep yourselves from idols. Amen.
23. To the only wise God our Saviour, be glory and majesty, dominion and power, both now and ever. Amen.
24. And were continually in the temple, praising and blessing God. Amen.
25. Teaching them to observe all things whatsoever I have commanded you: and, lo, I am with you alway, even unto the end of the world. Amen.
26. Yea, every pot in Jerusalem and in Judah shall be holiness unto the Lord of hosts.
27. And for the wood offering, at times appointed, and for the firstfruits. Remember me, O my God, for good.
28. And Obed begat Jesse, and Jesse begat David.
29. And Eleazar the son of Aaron died; and they buried him in a hill that pertained to Phinehas.
30. And they went forth, and preached every where, the Lord working with them, and confirming the word with signs following. Amen.

Five Pebbles and a Slingshot

How victorious could our soldiers be today if they used some of the weapons from Bible days! See if you can identify the items used as weapons below.

1. King Saul hurled it at David.
2. The young shepherd boy used this when he slew Goliath.
3. Although a very unusual weapon, Gideon used it to win a battle.
4. Joab thrust three of these through Absalom's heart.
5. In Gethsemane Peter used this to sever the servant's ear.
6. Saul's own weapon that he fell upon and killed himself.
7. Although not thought of as a weapon, it was used to take Haman's life.
8. Samson killed 1,000 men with this.
9. Heber's wife, Jael, plunged this into Sisera's head.
10. Joshua and all Israel used these to kill Achan.
11. King Zimri used this to kill himself.
12. Goliath carried these three things to fight the shepherd boy.
13. Shamgar used this to kill 600 Philistines.
14. David used these to kill both a lion and a bear.
15. The Word of God is compared to this weapon.
16. Although not really a weapon, it won a battle for a discouraged army.
17. Jonathan used this weapon as a warning to David.
18. Beniah killed an Egyptian man with this weapon.
19. Under the Law, this was used to kill a boy who disobeyed his parents.
20. The angel of God used this to keep Adam and Eve out of the Garden of Eden.

The Story of Christmas

The Christmas story is one of the best-known Bible stories. You probably are very familiar with it. The questions in this quiz have been taken from Luke's and Matthew's Gospels. You should find this quiz easy.

1. God sent this angel to inform Mary of the coming birth of her son. *Gabriel*
2. Nazareth was a city of this province. *Galilee*
3. Joseph was of this house and lineage. *David*
4. The angel instructed Mary to give her baby this name.
5. The child would reign over this house forever.
6. This elderly cousin of Mary's was also expecting a child. *Elizabeth*
7. A word both Mary's cousin and the angel used to describe Mary.
8. The length of Mary's stay with her cousin. *3 months*
9. The name given to Zacharias' and Elisabeth's son. *John*
10. This man decreed that all the world be taxed.
11. Joseph and Mary were required to go to this town to pay their taxes. *Bethlehem*
12. This word describes the clothes in which Mary wrapped her baby.
13. Who informed the shepherds of Jesus' birth? *angels*
14. This name means "God with us." *Emmanuel*
15. He was king of Judea at the time of Jesus' birth. *Herod*
16. The wise men followed it to Bethlehem. *star*
17. The three gifts brought by the wise men.
18. How was Joseph warned to flee into Egypt?
19. At what time did Joseph and his family flee the country? *at night*
20. How long was Joseph instructed to remain in Egypt? *until Herod died.*

Prayers of Mighty Warriors

Some of the men and women in the Bible are remembered for the prayers they gave. Can you identify the persons making the following petitions?

1. She prayed for a son and, while praying, was thought to be drunk.
2. He wrestled all night with an angel of God for his blessing.
3. He prayed that he would be permitted to see the Promised Land.
4. Asked that God would grant him understanding for his people.
5. He prayed for divine favor and enlightenment.
6. This man prayed for deliverance from a great fish.
7. He asked God for deliverance from the Assyrians.
8. To gain permission to escape to Zoar was this man's prayer.
9. This childless man prayed for an heir.
10. A king who prayed for healing from a dangerous illness.
11. They asked God's help and guidance in choosing an apostle to take Judas' place.
12. He asked Jesus to remember him when He was in His Kingdom.
13. A body of people who asked for boldness to preach the Word of God.
14. This people prayed for deliverance from bondage.
15. He prayed for strength to obtain vengeance on the Philistines.
16. He asked God to restore life to the widow's son.
17. He prayed for Dorcas to be brought back to life.
18. A body of people who prayed for Peter to be released from prison.
19. He prayed for Sodom and Gomorrah.
20. This man prayed that God would triumph over Baal.

The Ministry of Christ

Jesus spent the last three years of His life in public teaching. How much of that teaching do you know? If you can't answer these questions, you should reread the four Gospels.

1. Jesus said He came to call them to repentance.
2. Man shall not live by this alone.
3. You should do this to them that curse you.
4. This sin can never be forgiven, and he who commits it is in danger of eternal damnation.
5. A prophet is without it only in his own country, among his own kin, and in his own house.
6. These two things will pass away, but the Word of God will never pass away.
7. Jesus' disciples will be sent forth as these among the wolves.
8. The disciple is not above this person.
9. A man's foes shall be from here.
10. This is the light of the body.
11. Jesus commands us to seek this first.
12. It is of no good if it has lost its savour.
13. You can have anything accomplished if you have this much faith.
14. Jesus said the kingdom of God is here.
15. He that believeth on Christ will have it.
16. We must not judge according to this, but judge, instead, righteous judgment.
17. We shall abide in Jesus' love if we keep them.
18. Greater love hath no man than to do this.
19. What will it profit a man if he gains the whole world but loses this?
20. Except ye become as one of these, you shall not enter into the kingdom of heaven.
21. If you offend a child who believes in Jesus, it would be better for you to have this hung around your neck.
22. If one of these members of your body offends you, cut if off and cast it away.

23. If this member of your body offends you, pluck it out.
24. God is not the God of the dead but of the _____.
25. We will always have them with us.
26. If it is divided against itself, it cannot stand.
27. Forbid them not, for theirs is the kingdom of God.
28. It is easier for one of these to go through the eye of a needle than for a rich man to enter the kingdom of God.
29. Five of them can be purchased for two farthings.
30. We shouldn't fear because it is the Father's good pleasure to give it to us.

Answer Section

They Were Writers
1. Paul
2. Jeremiah
3. Luke
4. Job
5. Moses
6. Joshua
7. Ezra
8. Solomon
9. James
10. Peter
11. Hosea
12. David
13. Joshua
14. Jude
15. John
16. Amos
17. Peter
18. Paul
19. Isaiah
20. John

Teachings of the Beatitudes
1. c
2. f
3. a
4. h
5. d
6. g
7. b
8. c
9. e

Where Is It?
1. 1 Samuel
2. Acts
3. Esther
4. Genesis
5. Philemon
6. 1 Samuel
7. Matthew
8. Matthew
9. Acts
10. Luke
11. Exodus
12. 1 Corinthians
13. Genesis
14. Acts
15. Luke
16. Jonah
17. Daniel
18. 1 Samuel
19. Judges
20. 1 Samuel
21. Revelation
22. Matthew
23. John
24. Genesis
25. Exodus

The Psalms of David
1. Shepherd, Psalms 23:1
2. Lord, Psalms 8:9
3. Redeemer, Psalms 19:14
4. God, Psalms 63:1
5. King, Psalms 24:9
6. Refuge, Psalms 46:1
7. Shield, Psalms 3:3
8. Salvation, Psalms 27:1
9. Rock, Psalms 42:9
10. House, Psalms 31:2
11. Dwelling place, Psalms 90:1
12. Keeper, Psalms 121:5
13. Song, Psalms 118:14
14. Rock, fortress, deliverer, Psalms 18:2
15. Strength, Psalms, 28:8
16. Rock, Psalms 92:15
17. Sun, Psalms 84:11
18. King, Psalms 74:12
19. Judge, Psalms 75:7
20. Father, judge, Psalms 68:5

Professional Skills
1. Priscilla and Aquila
2. Luke
3. Paul
4. Zacchaeus
5. Peter
6. Gamaliel
7. Lydia
8. Philemon
9. Moses
10. Jochebed
11. Nimrod
12. David
13. Joseph
14. Dorcas
15. Cain
16. Joseph of Nazareth
17. Philip
18. Demetrius
19. Sergius Paulus
20. Joshua

It Was Romance
1. c
2. k
3. t
4. a
5. n
6. f
7. r
8. s
9. p
10. e
11. d
12. h
13. i
14. b
15. g
16. l
17. m
18. j
19. q
20. o

Categorize That Book
1. b
2. c
3. c
4. a
5. d
6. d
7. e
8. b
9. d
10. c
11. e
12. a
13. c
14. d
15. b
16. e
17. b
18. c
19. e
20. a
21. d
22. e
23. a
24. b
25. e

Kings and Queens
1. Jabin, Judges 4:2, 3
2. Darius, Daniel 6:1, 16
3. Saul, 1 Samuel 11:15
4. Esther, Esther 2:17
5. Elah, 1 Kings 16:8–10
6. Jezebel, 1 Kings 21:23
7. Candace, Acts 8:27
8. Bernice, Acts 25:13
9. David, 2 Samuel 19:16–18
10. Belshazzar, Daniel 5
11. Herodias, Matthew 14:3–8
12. Athaliah, 2 Kings 11:1
13. Joash, 2 Chronicles 24:1
14. Josiah, 2 Kings 22:1
15. Bathsheba, 2 Samuel 12:24

16. Maachah, 2 Chronicles 15:16
17. Hezekiah, 2 Kings 20:20
18. Solomon, 1 Kings 10:23
19. Queen of Sheba, 1 Kings 10:1
20. Ahab, 1 Kings 16:33

Who Am I?

1. Lot, Genesis 19:26
2. John the Baptist, Mark 6:27
3. Silas, Acts 16:25
4. Cain, Genesis 4:1
5. Saul, 1 Samuel 31:4
6. Judas, Matthew 26:14, 15
7. Isaiah, Isaiah 20:3
8. Mary, John 12:3
9. Jesus, John 13:3–5
10. Jacob, Genesis 37:34
11. John, Revelation 1:9
12. Jonathan, 1 Samuel 18:3
13. Rebekah, Genesis 24:61
14. Esau, Genesis 25:24–26
15. Saul, Acts 13:9
16. Abraham, Genesis 17:5
17. John, John 19:26
18. Gabriel, Luke 1:26, 27
19. Paul, Acts 20:9, 10
20. Moses, Exodus 3:1, 2
21. Martha, Luke 10:40
22. Peter, Matthew 26:75
23. Jesse, 1 Samuel 16:19
24. Miriam, Numbers 12:1–10
25. Lazarus, John 11:43
26. Haman, Esther 7:10
27. Michal, 1 Samuel 18:17–20
28. Noah, Genesis 6:8
29. Sarah, Genesis 16:1–3
30. God

Some Tricky Items

1. Maiden
2. Tent
3. Heat

4. Rest
5. Scribe
6. Farthing
7. Harp
8. Sheep
9. Ephod
10. Hall
11. Inn
12. Parables
13. Sword
14. Stoning
15. Stable
16. Flags
17. Den
18. Agape
19. Asp
20. Sundial
21. Hand staff
22. Ford
23. Beam
24. Balm

Dreams and Dreamers

1. e
2. a
3. c
4. f
5. b
6. h
7. i
8. d
9. f
10. c
11. a
12. g
13. k
14. j
15. l

What's That in Your Hand?

1. k
2. q
3. n
4. a
5. b
6. i

7. p
8. g
9. d
10. c
11. l
12. t
13. e
14. m
15. f
16. s
17. o
18. h
19. j
20. r

Remember the Trees?
1. Ash, Isaiah 44:13, 14
2. Cedar, Ezekiel 17:3–6
3. Myrtle, Zechariah 1:7–11
4. Pomegranate, 1 Samuel 14:2
5. Oak, 2 Samuel 18:9
6. Olive, Deuteronomy 24:20
7. Sycamore, Luke 19:4
8. Cedar, Ezekiel 17:1–6
9. Tree of Life, Genesis 3:22
10. Fir, 1 Kings 6:34
11. Palm, John 12:13
12. Bramble, Judges 9:14
13. Tree of Knowledge of Good and Evil, Genesis 2:9
14. Gopher, Genesis 6:14
15. Juniper, 1 Kings 19:4
16. Olive, Acts 1:12
17. Fig, Matthew 21:19
18. Cedar, 1 Kings 5:6
19. Mulberry, 2 Samuel 5:24
20. Willow, Psalms 137:1–4

They Were First
1. Adam
2. Eve
3. Cain
4. Flood

5. Enoch
6. River turned to blood
7. Rebekah
8. Cain
9. Nimrod
10. Abel
11. Moses
12. Cain
13. Aaron
14. Exodus 15
15. Ararat
16. Joseph
17. Rachel
18. Saul
19. Samuel
20. Simon
21. Paul
22. Antioch
23. Cana
24. Antioch
25. Stephen
26. Genesis
27. Matthew
28. Ezra
29. Ruth
30. Feeding of the 5,000

They Have Feathers
1. e
2. j
3. a
4. n
5. g
6. b
7. l
8. c
9. p
10. o
11. i
12. f
13. r
14. d
15. k
16. h

111

17. q
18. m

Hunter's Choice
1. Goat, Genesis 37:31–33
2. Dog, Proverbs 26:17
3. Cattle, Genesis 47:17
4. Swine, Mark 5:13
5. Bear or lion, 1 Samuel 17:36
6. Sheep
7. Ass
8. Camel, Mark 1:6
9. Viper, Acts 28:3
10. Foxes, Judges 15:4
11. Horse, Jeremiah 4:13
12. Lion, Micah 5:8
13. Calf, Exodus 32:4

Complete the Verse
1. Sting, victory
2. Strength, wings, weary, faint
3. Light, darkness, life
4. Heart
5. Created
6. Wept
7. House, mansions, prepare
8. Noise
9. Word, lamp, light, path
10. Confess, faithful, cleanse
11. Live, die, gain
12. Believe, house
13. Loved, love
14. Laugh, derision
15. Power, strength
16. Blood, sins
17. Commandments
18. All, strengtheneth
19. Ashamed, believed, committed
20. One, guilty
21. Refuge, fortress, trust
22. Fight, course, faith
23. Lord, praised, mountain
24. Refuge, strength, help
25. Chaff, wind

Who Said It?
1. Ruth
2. Jesus
3. David
4. Solomon
5. Paul
6. Jesus
7. Stephen
8. Cain
9. Jesus
10. Pilate
11. Centurion
12. John the Baptist
13. God
14. Martha
15. Thomas
16. Peter
17. Paul
18. John the Baptist
19. Nicodemus
20. Jesus
21. Paul
22. David
23. Job
24. Esther
25. Jesus

Name the Song
1. "Near the Cross"
2. "I Surrender All"
3. "Jewels"
4. "The Doxology"
5. "Let the Lower Lights Be Burning"
6. "The Lily of the Valley"
7. "Bringing in the Sheaves"
8. "Sweet Peace, the Gift of God's Love"
9. "May Jesus Christ Be Praised"
10. "Faith Is the Victory"

112

11. "Nothing but the Blood"
12. "My Saviour's Love"
13. "Jesus Saves"
14. "The Light of the World Is Jesus"
15. "I Know Whom I Have Believed"
16. "Wonderful Peace"
17. "Joy Unspeakable"
18. "Christ Arose"
19. "Hidden Peace"
20. "When We All Get to Heaven"
21. "Battle Hymn of the Republic"
22. "Trust and Obey"
23. "Higher Ground"
24. "It Is Mine"
25. "He Hideth My Soul"
26. "He Brought Me Out"
27. "I'll Go Where You Want Me to Go"
28. "There Is Power in the Blood"
29. "Sweet By and By"
30. "He Abides"
31. "Leaning on the Everlasting Arms"
32. "The Comforter Has Come"
33. "The Solid Rock"
34. "At the Cross"
35. "At Calvary"
36. "The Haven of Rest"
37. "It Is Well With My Soul"
38. "God Leads Us Along"
39. "A Child of the King"
40. "When the Roll Is Called Up Yonder"
41. "I've Anchored in Jesus"
42. "Revive Us Again"
43. "Satisfied"
44. "His Yoke Is Easy"
45. "I Know God's Promise Is True"

A Look at Mothers
1. Hannah
2. Hagar
3. Jochebed
4. Elisabeth
5. Mary
6. Eve
7. Sarah
8. Rebekah
9. Ruth
10. Bathsheba
11. Eve
12. Eunice
13. Herodias
14. Mary
15. Rebekah

What Did They Eat?
1. Daniel, Daniel 1:8–16
2. Locusts, Matthew 3:4
3. Manna, Exodus 16:15
4. Flour, Leviticus 5:11, 12
5. Sop, John 13:26
6. Fishes, Matthew 14:19
7. Vinegar, Mark 15:36
8. Oil, 1 Kings 17:8–16
9. Bread, Ezekiel 4:16
10. Corn
11. Loaves, 1 Samuel 17:17
12. Milk, Song of Solomon 5:1
13. Cheese, Job 10:10
14. Vegetarian, Daniel 1:11–15
15. Salt, Job 6:6
16. Honey, Judges 14:8, 9
17. Honey, 1 Samuel 14:24–27
18. Salt, Matthew 5:13
19. Bread, Matthew 6:11
20. Fish, John 21:6–9
21. Fig, Matthew 21:17–19

22. Honey, Matthew 3:4
23. Cake, Hosea 7:8
24. Mustard, Matthew 13:31
25. Ham, Genesis 5:32

April Fools' Day
1. f
2. n
3. a
4. t
5. k
6. c
7. h
8. r
9. b
10. o
11. d
12. i
13. l
14. g
15. j
16. e
17. m
18. q
19. s
20. p

A Look at Fathers
1. Abraham, Genesis 22:1–19
2. Jonathan, 2 Samuel 4:4
3. King Saul, 1 Samuel 19:1
4. Adam, Genesis 4:1
5. Zacharias, Luke 1:59–64
6. Joseph, Genesis 37:3
7. Laban, Genesis 29:16–25
8. Jairus, Mark 5:22, 23
9. God
10. Joseph
11. Noah, Genesis 7:7
12. Jesse, 1 Samuel 17:12
13. Isaac, Genesis 25:20–24
14. Moses, Exodus 14
15. Nun, Joshua 1:1
16. Manoah, Judges 13:21–24

17. Zebedee, Mark 1:19
18. David, 2 Samuel 12:24
19. Eli, 1 Samuel 3:12, 13
20. Aaron, Leviticus 10:6

New Testament Persons
1. Lydia, Acts 16:14, 15
2. Zebedee, Mark 1:19
3. Nicodemus, John 3:1, 2
4. Agrippa, Acts 26:28
5. Lazarus, John 11:1–46
6. Herod, Matthew 2:13
7. Rhoda, Acts 12:13
8. Nicodemus, John 7:50, 51
9. Thomas, John 20:25
10. Lazarus, Luke 16:20–31
11. James, Matthew 17:1
12. Mary Magdalene, Mark 16:9
13. Matthew (or Levi), Mark 2:14, 15
14. Paul, Acts 9:24, 25
15. Mary, John 11:1
16. Paul, Acts 17:22
17. Peter, Acts 2:14–41
18. Stephen, Acts 7:57–59
19. Peter, Acts 12:7
20. Jesus, Luke 4:29

Old Testament Persons
1. Jezebel, 1 Kings 18:4
2. Delilah, Judges 16:18–20
3. Eli, 1 Samuel 4:16–18
4. Elijah, 1 Kings 18:42–44
5. Amon, 2 Kings 21:19–23
6. Abner, 1 Samuel 14:50, 51
7. Vashti, Esther 1:12
8. Asahel, 2 Samuel 2:18
9. Gehazi, 2 Kings 5:20–27
10. Deborah, Judges 4:4, 5
11. Abraham, Genesis 17:5–8
12. Haman, Esther 3:1, 6
13. Enoch, Genesis 5:24
14. Jonah, Jonah 1:1–6
15. Michal, 2 Samuel 6:16

16. Moses, Exodus 3:4, 5
17. Mephibosheth, 2 Samuel 9:6, 7
18. Samson, Judges 15:7–14
19. Goliath, 1 Samuel 17:22–58
20. Rebekah, Genesis 24:15–19

Summarize the Books
1. Ruth
2. Psalms
3. Leviticus
4. Haggai
5. Song of Solomon
6. 2 Samuel
7. Genesis
8. Joshua
9. Numbers
10. 1 Samuel
11. Job
12. Daniel
13. Zephaniah
14. Nahum
15. Amos
16. Lamentations
17. Jonah
18. Malachi
19. Esther
20. Proverbs

Just Kinfolk
1. Father
2. Wife
3. Grandmother
4. Great-grandson
5. Great-uncle
6. Sister-in-law
7. Sister
8. Father-in-law
9. Brother
10. Daughter
11. Mother
12. Cousin
13. Son

14. Wife
15. Father
16. Uncle
17. Niece
18. Son-in-law
19. Brother
20. Mother-in-law
21. Son
22. Father
23. Nephew
24. Brother

Please Tell Me the Name
1. Simon, Mark 3:16
2. Abram, Genesis 17:5
3. Iscariot, Matthew 10:4
4. John, Acts 15:37
5. Saul, Acts 13:9
6. Sarai, Genesis 17:15
7. Tabitha, Acts 9:36
8. Belteshazzar, Daniel 10:1
9. Hadassah, Esther 2:7
10. Israel, Genesis 32:28
11. The Baptist, Matthew 3:1
12. The Tishbite, 1 Kings 17:1
13. Didymus, John 11:16
14. Jerubbaal, Judges 6:28–32
15. The Gittite, 1 Chronicles 20:5
16. Mara, Ruth 1:20
17. Levi, Luke 5:27–29
18. Joses, Acts 4:36
19. Jedidiah, 2 Samuel 12:24, 25
20. Barsabas, Acts 1:23

Their Names Had Meanings
1. e
2. a
3. i
4. f
5. o
6. k
7. c
8. g

115

9. b
10. d
11. y
12. m
13. q
14. s
15. h
16. v
17. l
18. r
19. x
20. p
21. t
22. n
23. u
24. w
25. j

Explain the Meaning
1. b
2. d
3. a
4. e
5. c
6. g
7. f

How Did They Travel?
1. Chariot, 2 Kings 2:11
2. Camels
3. Donkey
4. Horses
5. Ship, Acts 27:15–44
6. Chariot, 2 Kings 9:16
7. Caravans
8. Donkey
9. On foot
10. Camels, Genesis 24:10–33
11. Ark, Genesis 8:4
12. Fish, Jonah 1:17
13. Basket, Acts 9:25
14. Chariot, Acts 8:28
15. Bed, Matthew 9:2
16. Colt, Matthew 21:2
17. Mule, 2 Samuel 18:9

18. Horse, Esther 6:11
19. Wagons, Genesis 45:17–19

An Alphabet of Cities and Places
1. Antioch, Acts 11:19–30
2. Bethlehem, Luke 2:4
3. Capernaum, Matthew 4:13
4. Damascus, 1 Kings 20:34
5. Enoch, Genesis 4:17
6. Fortress, 2 Samuel 22:2
7. Galilee, Acts 1:11
8. Hell, Matthew 11:23
9. Iconium, Acts 13:51
10. Jerusalem, 1 Chronicles 11:4–7
11. Kedesh, Joshua 12:22
12. Lystra, 2 Timothy 3:11
13. Macedonia, Acts 16:9
14. Nod, Genesis 4:16
15. Ophni, Joshua 18:24
16. Paphos, Acts 13:6–13
17. Rome, Romans 1:15
18. Samaria, John 4:4
19. Tarsus, Acts 9:11
20. Ur of the Chaldees, Genesis 11:28
21. Valley, Luke 3:5
22. Wilderness, Numbers 14:20–39

From Ashes to Victory
1. Uz, Job 1:1
2. Ten, Job 1:2
3. 11,000, Job 1:3
4. Satan, Job 1:7
5. Perfect and upright, Job 1:8
6. Oxen and asses, Job 1:14, 15
7. Chaldeans, Job 1:17
8. Take Job's life, Job 2:6
9. Boils, Job 2:7

116

10. Ashes, Job 2:8
11. Eliphaz, Bildad, and Zophar, Job 2:11
12. To mourn with him and to comfort him, Job 2:11
13. Seven days and seven nights, Job 2:13
14. Prey, Job 4:11
15. Wrath, Job 5:2
16. The sand of the sea, Job 6:3
17. Worms and clods of dust, Job 7:5
18. Trouble, Job 14:1
19. Miserable, Job 16:2
20. Death, Job 16:16
21. Ten, Job 42:13
22. 22,000, Job 42:12
23. Jemima, Job 42:14
24. 140, Job 42:16
25. Four, Job 42:16

Those Sparkling Gems

1. Gold, 2 Chronicles 9:20
2. Emerald, Exodus 28:15–18
3. Sapphire, Revelation 21:19
4. Diamond, Exodus 28:18
5. Salt, Genesis 19:26
6. Pearl, Matthew 13:46
7. Brimstone, Genesis 19:24
8. Ivory, 1 Kings 22:39
9. Silver, Matthew 26:15
10. Alabaster, Matthew 26:7
11. Iron, Acts 12:10
12. Topaz, Job 28:19

The Flutter of Angels' Wings

1. Assyrian, 2 Kings 19:35
2. Elisha, 2 Kings 6:14–17
3. Zacharias, Luke 1:13
4. Twelve, Matthew 26:53
5. Michael, Daniel 10:13
6. Jacob's, Genesis 28:10–12

7. Abraham, Genesis 18:1–10
8. Cornelius, Acts 10:3
9. Jacob, Hosea 12:4
10. Jesus, Matthew 4:11
11. Gabriel, Luke 1:19; Michael, Jude 9; Apollyon, Revelation 9:11
12. Michael, Jude 9
13. Herod, Acts 12:23
14. Guardian, Matthew 18:10
15. Gideon, Judges 6:19, 20
16. Paul, Acts 27:23
17. Manoah, Judges 13:15, 16
18. Sodom, Genesis 19:15–24
19. Jesus, Acts 1:10
20. Elijah, 1 Kings 19:5–7
21. Hagar, Genesis 16:7, 8
22. Gabriel, Luke 1:26–33
23. Reapers, Matthew 13:39
24. Michael, 1 Thessalonians 4:16
25. Isaac's, Genesis 22:11, 12
26. Shepherds, Luke 2:8–15
27. Two, John 20:11–14
28. Evil, Matthew 25:41
29. Marriage, Genesis 24:7
30. Idolatry, Judges 2:1–5

So Much Symbolism

1. d
2. g
3. i
4. f
5. a
6. h
7. b
8. j
9. e
10. c
11. n
12. q
13. l
14. o

15. t
16. r
17. y
18. k
19. w
20. u
21. m
22. s
23. p
24. x
25. v

There's No *A* in *Quiz*
1. Ahab, 1 Kings 16:29–33
2. Aaron, Exodus 40:13–16
3. Athaliah, 2 Kings 11:1
4. Abed-nego, Daniel 1:7
5. Amaziah, 2 Chronicles 25:1–3
6. Augustus, Luke 2:1
7. Athens, Acts 17:22
8. Abigail, 1 Samuel 25:3–44
9. Agag, 1 Samuel 15:9–33
10. Anna, Luke 2:36–38
11. Annunciation
12. Ascension, Acts 1:1–12

How Many Were There?
1. Twelve, Luke 6:13
2. Thirteen, Joshua 6
3. Seventy times seven, Matthew 18:21, 22
4. Ninety-nine, Matthew 18:12
5. Three
6. Twelve, Matthew 14:20
7. Two, Joshua 2:1
8. Three, Jonah 1:17
9. One year, Genesis 7, 8
10. Four, Daniel 3:20–25
11. Thirty, Matthew 26:14–16
12. Seven, 2 Kings 11:21
13. Three, Daniel 6:10
14. Fourteen, Genesis 29:15–30
15. Ten, Luke 17:12–14
16. Twenty-seven
17. Thirty-nine
18. Ten, Genesis 24:10
19. Twenty, Genesis 37:28
20. Seven hundred, Judges 20:16

Tell Me the Author
1. d
2. e
3. c
4. j
5. a
6. a
7. h
8. l
9. b
10. i
11. a
12. f
13. h
14. c
15. m
16. k
17. c
18. c
19. c
20. b
21. a
22. n
23. f
24. c
25. f

Water, Water, Water
1. c
2. i
3. e
4. j
5. a
6. k
7. g
8. f
9. f

10. f
11. b
12. d
13. h
14. h
15. l
16. o
17. n
18. h
19. m
20. p
21. r
22. t
23. q
24. s
25. j

Just Hair
1. d
2. a
3. f
4. d
5. b
6. c
7. i
8. h
9. e
10. b
11. g

Blessed Are They
1. Law, Psalms 1:2
2. Judgment, Psalms 106:3
3. Chasten, Psalms 94:12
4. Dwell, Psalms 84:4
5. Strength, Psalms 84:5
6. Poor, Psalms 41:1
7. Trust, Psalms 40:4
8. Forgiven, Psalms 32:1
9. Lord, Psalms 33:12
10. Iniquity, Psalms 32:2
11. Courts, Psalms 65:4
12. Name, Psalms 118:26
13. Testimonies, Psalms 119:2
14. Ungodly, Psalms 1:1

15. Feareth, Psalms 128:1
16. Choosest, Psalms 65:4
17. Joyful, Psalms 89:15
18. Undefiled, Psalms 119:1
19. Trusteth, Psalms 34:8
20. Trust, Psalms 2:12

Biblical Facts That Are Nice to Know
1. Old Testament and New Testament
2. Thirty-nine
3. Twenty-seven
4. Sixty-six
5. Law, history, poetry, major prophets, minor prophets
6. Biography, history, special letters, general letters, prophecy
7. Apocalypse
8. Greek
9. The four Gospels
10. Acts
11. Revelation
12. Psalms 118:8
13. Psalms
14. Esther 8:9
15. John 11:35
16. Psalms 117
17. Psalms 119
18. Proverbs
19. 2 Kings 19 and Isaiah 37
20. 1,189

They Performed Miracles
1. Ananias, Acts 9:18
2. Peter, Acts 9:36–42
3. Moses, Exodus 14:21, 22
4. Gabriel, Luke 1:11–23
5. Elijah, 1 Kings 17:10–14
6. Joshua, Joshua 10:12, 13
7. Jesus, Mark 4:37–41
8. Elisha, 2 Kings 6:6
9. Paul, Acts 13:6–11

10. Moses, Exodus 7:10
11. Elisha, 2 Kings 4:32–36
12. Elisha, 2 Kings 6:17
13. Jesus, Luke 22:51
14. Peter, Acts 3:7
15. Jesus, Luke 4:39
16. Angel, Acts 12:7–10
17. Paul, Acts 16:18
18. Joshua, Joshua 6:20
19. Elisha, 2 Kings 2:14
20. Jesus, John 5:1–9
21. Jesus, John 2:1–11
22. Elisha, 2 Kings 5:1–19
23. Paul, Acts 28:5
24. Jesus, Matthew 12:9–13
25. Jesus, John 9

Identify the Word
1. a
2. b
3. a
4. c
5. a
6. c
7. a
8. c
9. c
10. c
11. a
12. b
13. a
14. b
15. b
16. c
17. c
18. b
19. b
20. a
21. c
22. b
23. a
24. c
25. b
26. c

27. c
28. a
29. c
30. d
31. c
32. c
33. a
34. a
35. d

Scriptural Anatomy
1. Heart, 1 Samuel 16:7
2. Eye, Matthew 5:29
3. Feet, John 13:4–14
4. Necks, Acts 7:51
5. Head, Acts 21:24
6. Heart, Proverbs 14:30
7. Neck, 1 Samuel 4:18
8. Fingers and toes, 2 Samuel 21:20–22
9. Teeth, Proverbs 30:14
10. Heart, Psalms 51:10
11. Feet, 2 Samuel 4:4
12. Eyes, Judges 16:21–31
13. Thigh, Genesis 32
14. Ear, Matthew 26:51
15. Hand, Acts 28:3–6
16. Head, 1 Samuel 17
17. Hand, Matthew 12:9–13
18. Body, Job 4:19
19. Side, John 19:34
20. Heart, Psalms 22:26
21. Head, Matthew 14:8
22. Face, Exodus 33:20
23. Hair, Judges 16:19
24. Hand, Exodus 4:6
25. Nose, Genesis 2:7
26. Tongue, James 3:5, 6
27. Back, Exodus 33:23
28. Cheek, Matthew 5:39

Similes in the Proverbs
1. h, Proverbs 12:4
2. a, Proverbs 16:31
3. b, Proverbs 14:8

120

4. m, Proverbs 17:22
5. t, Proverbs 4:18
6. d, Proverbs 4:19
7. q, Proverbs 19:12
8. e, Proverbs 25:11
9. k, Proverbs 19:12
10. i, Proverbs 27:15
11. c, Proverbs 25:25
12. o, Proverbs 6:34
13. v, Proverbs 11:30
14. y, Proverbs 11:22
15. r, Proverbs 9:10
16. j, Proverbs 18:4
17. l, Proverbs 18:4
18. w, Proverbs 20:17
19. p, Proverbs 22:14
20. n, Proverbs 25:12
21. s, Proverbs 9:17
22. f, Proverbs 16:32
23. g, Proverbs 25:28
24. x, Proverbs 25:18
25. u, Proverbs 25:13

Admonishments to Heed
1. d, Proverbs 22:24
2. a, Ecclesiastes 12:1
3. k, Proverbs 3:6
4. g, 2 Timothy 2:15
5. m, 1 Thessalonians 5:17
6. p, Proverbs 3:5
7. c, Isaiah 40:31
8. f, 1 Timothy 5:1
9. t, John 13:34
10. h, Luke 18:1
11. l, Proverbs 3:3
12. n, Matthew 5:16
13. b, Luke 6:37
14. e, Mark 13:33
15. o, Ephesians 6:10
16. q, Ephesians 4:26
17. s, Ephesians 4:29
18. r, 1 Thessalonians 5:18
19. j, Colossians 3:2
20. i, James 5:16

From Shepherd to King
1. Jesse, 1 Samuel 16:1
2. Samuel, 1 Samuel 16:1–4
3. Eight, 1 Samuel 16:10, 11
4. Forty, 1 Samuel 17:16
5. Lion and bear, 1 Samuel 17:34
6. Brook, 1 Samuel 17:40
7. One, 1 Samuel 17:49, 50
8. Jonathan, 1 Samuel 18:1
9. Twice, 1 Samuel 18:11
10. Michal, 1 Samuel 18:20, 21
11. Samuel, 1 Samuel 19:18
12. Covenant, 1 Samuel 20:16
13. 3,000, 1 Samuel 24:2
14. Abigail, 1 Samuel 25:1–19
15. Ziklag, 1 Samuel 27:5, 6
16. Bathsheba, 2 Samuel 11:2, 3
17. Uriah, 2 Samuel 11:15
18. Nathan, 2 Samuel 12:1–12
19. Bathsheba, 1 Kings 1:11
20. Solomon, 1 Kings 1:32–35

The Name, Sir? 'Tis Paul
1. Stephen, Acts 7:58–60
2. Jerusalem, Acts 8:1
3. Judea and Samaria, Acts 8:1
4. Damascus, Acts 9:2
5. Straight, Acts 9:11
6. Ananias, Acts 9:10
7. Jews, Acts 9:23–25
8. Barnabas, Acts 11:30
9. Mercurius, Acts 14:8–12
10. Antioch and Iconium, Acts 14:1–19
11. John Mark, Acts 15:37–39
12. Silas, Acts 15:40
13. Lydia, Acts 16:14, 15
14. Timothy, 1 Timothy 1:2
15. Eutychus, Acts 20:9

16. Two hundred and seventy-six, Acts 27:37
17. Melita, Acts 28:1
18. Cold and rainy, Acts 28:2
19. Viper, Acts 28:3, 4
20. Publius, Acts 28:7
21. Gentiles, Ephesians 3:1
22. Philemon, Philemon 1:1
23. Onesimus, Philemon 1:10
24. Brother beloved, Philemon 1:16
25. Paul had confidence in Philemon's obedience, Philemon 1:21

Principal Thoughts
1. Job
2. 1 Kings
3. 1 Chronicles
4. Jonah
5. Genesis
6. Leviticus
7. Nehemiah
8. Joshua
9. Psalms
10. Isaiah
11. Esther
12. Joel
13. Nahum
14. Matthew
15. Acts
16. Colossians
17. Mark
18. 1 and 2 Thessalonians
19. Luke
20. John
21. Philemon
22. Revelation
23. Romans
24. James
25. Galatians

Complete the Scripture
1. d, Matthew 11:29
2. h, Acts 2:38
3. l, Ecclesiastes 12:13
4. a, James 4:7
5. t, John 1:29
6. b, Isaiah 1:18
7. e, Galatians 6:7
8. o, Exodus 20:8
9. r, Acts 20:35
10. m, Numbers 32:23
11. i, Ezekiel 37:3
12. f, Psalms 46:1
13. k, Proverbs 15:1
14. q, Proverbs 16:18
15. n, Romans 6:23
16. c, Revelation 2:10
17. g, John 6:37
18. j, Proverbs 21:17
19. p, Isaiah 5:11
20. s, Song of Solomon 2:1

And the Songwriter Is . . .
1. b
2. d
3. b
4. c
5. b
6. d
7. e
8. d
9. c
10. c and a
11. b
12. c
13. c
14. b
15. b
16. d
17. c
18. b
19. b
20. c
21. d

22. d
23. e
24. d
25. c
26. d
27. b
28. b
29. c
30. b

Winged Insects
1. Locusts, Matthew 3:4
2. Hornets, Exodus 23:28
3. Gnats, Matthew 23:24
4. Ants, Proverbs 6:6–8
5. Lice, Exodus 8:16
6. Moth, Job 27:18
7. Spider's web, Job 8:14
8. Flies, Exodus 8:24
9. Bees, Psalms 118:12
10. Flies, Ecclesiastes 10:1
11. Grasshoppers, Judges 6:3–5
12. Fleas, 1 Samuel 24:14

What's In a *B*?
1. Boaz, Ruth 4:8–10
2. Barnabas, Acts 4:36, 37
3. Barley, 2 Samuel 14:30
4. Bethesda, John 5:2–8
5. Bear, 2 Samuel 17:8
6. Balaam, Numbers 22:31, 32
7. Babylonians, Psalms 137:3
8. Benjamin, Genesis 44:11, 12
9. Barrel, 1 Kings 17:12
10. Blastus, Acts 12:20
11. Brick, Exodus 1:14
12. Byways, Judges 5:6
13. Bildad, Job 2:11
14. Bit, Psalms 32:9
15. Birds, Genesis 1:20–23
16. Bethsaida, Mark 6:45
17. Bera, Genesis 14:2
18. Bethany, Mark 11:1–11
19. Beheaded, Acts 12:2
20. Baptism, Matthew 28:19
21. Barabbas, Matthew 27:16–26
22. Balm, Genesis 37:25
23. Babylon, Ezekiel 12:13
24. Ben-hail, 2 Chronicles 17:7
25. Benjamin, Genesis 35:18
26. Bernice, Acts 25:13
27. Bread, Ezekiel 4:16
28. Butter, Proverbs 30:33

Which One?
1. c, Genesis 29:16–28
2. b, Exodus 7:20
3. c, Numbers 3:2
4. a, Esther 1:11, 12
5. b, John 7:50
6. b, Joel 1:1
7. a, 2 Samuel 21:1
8. c, 1 Samuel 25:1
9. b, Genesis 23:1
10. b, 1 Kings 18:4
11. a, Esther 2:15, 16
12. a, Acts 1:23–26
13. b, 2 Timothy 4:13
14. a, Acts 13:8–11
15. c, 1 Chronicles 23:14
16. b, 2 Chronicles 9:1
17. c, Genesis 1:21–23
18. b, Genesis 6:8
19. c, Genesis 37:21
20. a, Genesis 37:28
21. c, Acts 16:9
22. a, Hebrews 11:1
23. b, Matthew 26:57
24. a, Psalms 68:17
25. b, Jonah 1:3
26. a, 1 Chronicles 10:2
27. a, Judges 15:18, 19
28. c, Acts 19:24

29. b, Revelation 3:14, 15
30. a, Acts 9:36

Name the Mary
1. b, Mark 16:9
2. c, John 12:1–3
3. a, Luke 1:27–36
4. d, Acts 12:12
5. b, John 20:1, 2
6. c, Luke 10:38–42
7. d, Acts 12:13
8. a, Luke 2:41
9. d, Colossians 4:10
10. b, Mark 16:9
11. b, Luke 8:1, 2
12. c, John 11:20–44
13. a, John 2:1–10
14. a, John 19:25–27
15. c, Luke 10:40

Jesus' Sermon on the Mount
1. Judgment, Matthew 5:22
2. Adultery, Matthew 5:28
3. Throne, Matthew 5:34
4. Footstool, Matthew 5:35
5. Hairs on your head, Matthew 5:36
6. Cloak, Matthew 5:40
7. Enemies, Matthew 5:44
8. Curse you, Matthew 5:44
9. Love, Matthew 5:44
10. Pray, Matthew 5:44
11. Sun, Matthew 5:45
12. Rain, Matthew 5:45
13. Hypocrites, Matthew 6:16
14. Masters, Matthew 6:24
15. Fowls of the air, Matthew 6:26
16. Lilies of the field, Matthew 6:28, 29
17. The kingdom of God, Matthew 6:33
18. Beam, Matthew 7:5
19. Pearls, Matthew 7:6
20. Wide, broad, Matthew 7:13
21. Straight, narrow, Matthew 7:14
22. False prophets, Matthew 7:15
23. Fruits, Matthew 7:20
24. Rock, Matthew 7:24, 25
25. Sand, Matthew 7:26, 27

Who Was Called?
1. Luke, Colossians 4:14
2. James and John, Mark 3:17
3. Abraham, James 2:23
4. David, 1 Samuel 13:14
5. Balaam, Numbers 24:3
6. Jacob, Genesis 27:36
7. Moses, Numbers 12:3
8. Barnabas, Acts 11:22–24
9. David, 2 Samuel 23:1
10. Thomas, John 20:25
11. Peter, Matthew 16:18
12. Judas, Mark 26:47–50
13. Mary, Luke 1:27
14. Gideon, Judges 6:12, 13
15. Jeremiah
16. John, John 13:23
17. Stephen, Acts 7
18. Luke
19. Cain, Genesis 4:14
20. Micah

A Bit of Everything
1. Mephibosheth, 2 Samuel 4:4
2. Absalom, 2 Samuel 18:9
3. Enoch, Genesis 5:18–24
4. Miriam, Numbers 12
5. Rebekah, Genesis 24:15–19
6. Eli, 1 Samuel 4:18
7. Esau, Genesis 25:25
8. Luke, Colossians 4:14
9. John, Revelation 1:9

10. James, Acts 12:2
11. Rebekah, Genesis 24:65
12. Solomon, 1 Kings 11:1–3
13. Jezebel, 2 Kings 9:30–37
14. Malchus, John 18:10
15. Peter, Matthew 10:2
16. David, 1 Samuel 16:12
17. Michael the archangel, 1 Thessalonians 4:16
18. Elijah, 1 Kings 18:24–38
19. Saul, 1 Samuel 31:4
20. Achan, Joshua 7:24

Fifty Questions About Jesus
1. Emmanuel, Matthew 1:23
2. Mary, Matthew 1:18
3. Herod, Matthew 2:1
4. Egypt, Matthew 2:14
5. Star, Matthew 2:2
6. Archelaus, Matthew 2:22
7. Nazareth, Matthew 2:23
8. John the Baptist, Mark 1:4
9. Forty, Mark 1:13
10. Holy Spirit, Mark 1:8
11. Dove, Mark 1:10
12. Twelve, Luke 6:12–19
13. Beatitudes, Matthew 5:3–11
14. Bethlehem, Luke 2:4–6
15. Herod, Matthew 2:7, 8
16. Cana, John 2:1–11
17. Peter, Matthew 14:29
18. Barabbas, Luke 23:18–24
19. Siloam, John 9:7
20. 153, John 21:11
21. Jairus, Luke 8:41–56
22. Two, Mark 12:29–31
23. House of prayer, Mark 11:17
24. Bethany, Matthew 26:6
25. Pilate, Matthew 27:2
26. Jacob's well, John 4:5–14
27. His Father's, John 5:43

28. Barley, John 6:9
29. Light, John 12:46
30. Scourging, John 19:1
31. Command stones to be made bread, Matthew 4:3
32. Hairs of our head, Matthew 10:30
33. Nazarene, Matthew 2:23
34. Bethany, Mark 14:1–25
35. Sang a hymn, Mark 14:26
36. Simon of Cyrene, Mark 15:21
37. Elias, Mark 15:34
38. To anoint the body with sweet spices, Mark 16:1
39. Frankincense, Matthew 2:11
40. Peter, James, and John, Matthew 17:1
41. Moses and Elijah, Matthew 17:3
42. Pharisees, Matthew 22:15–22
43. Hypocrites, Matthew 22:18
44. Sadducees, Matthew 22:23–33
45. John the Baptist, Mark 6:14
46. He made the deaf to hear and the dumb speak, Mark 7:37
47. Simon Peter, Mark 14:37
48. Twice, Mark 14:72
49. Veil, Mark 15:38
50. Bethany, Luke 24:50, 51

An Alphabet Quiz
1. Aaron
2. Bethlehem
3. Cana
4. David
5. Enoch
6. Fig tree

7. Golgotha
8. Hagar
9. Isaac
10. Jerusalem
11. King
12. Lebanon
13. Matthew
14. Nicodemus
15. Onesimus
16. Patmos
17. Queen
18. Ruth
19. Samaria
20. Timothy
21. Uzziah
22. Veil
23. Wilderness
24. Xerxes
25. Zacchaeus

Find the Verse
1. h
2. d
3. a
4. k
5. c
6. f
7. n
8. i
9. l
10. e
11. m
12. g
13. o
14. j
15. b

Where, Oh, Where
1. Nineveh, Jonah 1:2
2. Cana, John 2:1, 2
3. Sheba, 1 Kings 10:1
4. Bethlehem, Luke 2:4, 5
5. Jerusalem, Matthew 21:9-11

6. Garden of Eden, Genesis 2:8
7. Haran, Genesis 28:10, 11
8. Nile, Exodus 2:2-6
9. Moab, Ruth 1:1-19
10. Nebo, Deuteronomy 34:1
11. Patmos, Revelation 1:9
12. Olives, Luke 22:39
13. Jerusalem, Matthew 23:37
14. Galilee, Luke 5:1
15. Sodom and Gomorrah, Genesis 19:24-26
16. Padanaram, Genesis 28:1-5
17. Shinar, Genesis 11:2-4
18. Shiloh, 1 Samuel 1:1-3
19. Judah and Jerusalem, Isaiah 1:1
20. Ishtob, 2 Samuel 10:6-8
21. Sychar, John 4:5, 6
22. En-dor, 1 Samuel 28:7
23. Dothan, Genesis 37:17-20
24. Joppa, Jonah 1:3
25. Gath, 1 Samuel 17:4
26. Elah, 1 Samuel 17:19
27. Damascus, 2 Corinthians 11:32, 33
28. Joppa, Acts 9:36
29. Golgotha, Matthew 27:33
30. Rock of Rimmon, Judges 20:47
31. Capernaum, Matthew 4:12, 13
32. Jericho, Joshua 6:1-20
33. Egypt, Genesis 41:41
34. Athens, Acts 17:22
35. Jerusalem, Acts 2:4, 5

Alpha
1. Psalms
2. Matthew
3. 2 John
4. Genesis
5. 1 Chronicles

6. Deuteronomy
7. 1 Kings
8. Hebrews
9. Acts
10. Daniel
11. Ecclesiastes
12. Job
13. 2 Kings
14. John
15. Exodus
16. Mark
17. Luke
18. Numbers

Omega
1. Judges
2. Nahum
3. Psalms
4. Revelation
5. 2 Samuel
6. Exodus
7. Genesis
8. Hosea
9. Lamentations
10. Isaiah
11. John
12. Proverbs
13. Esther
14. Ezra
15. 1 Chronicles
16. Song of Solomon
17. 2 Chronicles
18. Numbers
19. Ezekiel
20. Acts
21. James
22. 1 John
23. Jude
24. Luke
25. Matthew
26. Zechariah
27. Nehemiah
28. Ruth

29. Joshua
30. Mark

Five Pebbles and a Slingshot
1. Javelin, 1 Samuel 18:11
2. Sling, 1 Samuel 17:40–50
3. Trumpet, Judges 7:16–21
4. Darts, 2 Samuel 18:14
5. Sword, John 18:10
6. Sword, 1 Chronicles 10:4
7. Gallows, Esther 8:7
8. Jawbone of an ass, Judges 15:16
9. Nail, Judges 4:17–22
10. Stones, Joshua 7:24, 25
11. Fire, 1 Kings 16:18
12. Sword, shield, and spear, 1 Samuel 17:4–45
13. Ox goad, Judges 3:31
14. Hands, 1 Samuel 17:34–37
15. Two-edged sword, Hebrews 4:12
16. Thunder, 1 Samuel 7:7–11
17. Arrow, 1 Samuel 20:18–22
18. Spear, 2 Samuel 23:20, 21
19. Stones, Deuteronomy 21:18–21
20. Flaming sword, Genesis 3:24

The Story of Christmas
1. Gabriel, Luke 1:26, 27
2. Galilee, Luke 1:26
3. David, Luke 1:27
4. Jesus, Luke 1:31
5. Jacob, Luke 1:33
6. Elisabeth, Luke 1:36
7. Blessed, Luke 1:28, 42
8. Three months, Luke 1:56
9. John, Luke 1:63
10. Caesar Augustus, Luke 2:1
11. Bethlehem, Luke 2:4
12. Swaddling, Luke 2:7
13. Angels, Luke 2:8–13

14. Emmanuel, Matthew 1:23
15. Herod, Matthew 2:1
16. Star, Matthew 2:1–9
17. Gold, frankincense, and myrrh, Matthew 2:11
18. By an angel in a dream, Matthew 2:13
19. During the night, Matthew 2:14
20. Until Herod was dead, Matthew 2:13–20

Prayers of Mighty Warriors
1. Hannah, 1 Samuel 1:10–28
2. Jacob, Genesis 32:24–30
3. Moses, Deuteronomy 3:25
4. Solomon, 1 Kings 3:6–14
5. Cornelius, Acts 10:1–4
6. Jonah, Jonah 2
7. Manasseh, 2 Chronicles 33:11–13
8. Lot, Genesis 19:18–22
9. Abram, Genesis 15:1–6
10. Hezekiah, 2 Kings 20
11. The apostles, Acts 1:15–26
12. The crucified thief, Luke 23:42, 43
13. Church, Acts 4:23–31
14. Israelites, Exodus 2:23–25
15. Samson, Judges 16:28–30
16. Elijah, 1 Kings 17:20–23
17. Peter, Acts 9:36–40
18. Church, Acts 12:1–12
19. Abraham, Genesis 18.20–32
20. Elijah, 1 Kings 18:36–38

The Ministry of Christ
1. Sinners, Matthew 9:13
2. Bread, Matthew 4:4

3. Bless, Matthew 5:44
4. Blasphemy against the Holy Ghost, Mark 3:29
5. Honor, Mark 6:4
6. Heaven and earth, Mark 13:31
7. Sheep, Matthew 10:16
8. Master, Matthew 10:24
9. His own household, Matthew 10:36
10. Eye, Luke 11:34
11. The kingdom of God, Luke 12:31
12. Salt, Matthew 5:13
13. Faith as a grain of mustard seed, Luke 17:6
14. Within you, Luke 17:21
15. Everlasting life, John 6:47
16. Appearance, John 7:24
17. Commandments, John 15:10
18. Lay down his life for his friends, John 15:13
19. His own soul, Matthew 16:26
20. Children, Matthew 18:3
21. Millstone, Matthew 18:6
22. Hand or foot, Matthew 18:8
23. Eye, Matthew 18:9
24. Living, Matthew 22:32
25. The poor, Matthew 26:11
26. House, Mark 3:25
27. Children, Mark 10:14
28. Camel, Mark 10:25
29. Sparrows, Luke 12:6
30. The kingdom, Luke 12:32